THE BOOK OF ACTS

THE BOOK OF

Acts

William R. Cannon

UPPER
ROOM BOOKS
NASHVILLE

THE BOOK OF ACTS

Scripture quotations not otherwise identified are from the King James Version of the Bible.

Scripture quotations designated RSV are from the Revised Standard Version of the Bible, copyrighted 1946, 1952, and © 1971 by the Division of Christian Education, National Council of Churches of Christ in America, and are used by permission.

Scripture quotations designated AP are the author's paraphrase.

Quotations from *The New Testament in Modern English*, by J. B. Phillips, are reprinted by permission of the Macmillan Company. Copyright © 1958 by J. B. Phillips.

Cover Design: Jim Bateman
First Printing: February 1989 (5)
Library of Congress Catalog Card Number: 88-051472
ISBN: 0-8358-0592-1

Printed in the United States of America

To

DOCTOR JAMES T. LANEY,

President of Emory University,

and

DOCTOR JIM L. WAITS,

Dean of the Candler School of Theology

of

Emory University,

with gratitude for enabling me to renew my teaching ministry

CONTENTS

PREFACE

THERE IS A plethora of commentaries on the Acts of the Apostles. Most of them, however, are exegetical in character and designed for ministers and theological students seeking a detailed understanding of the text. They deal with one verse at a time, examining it in the light of the meaning of each word and trying to discern the intention of the author in his use of the word. This book, in contrast, is written for the general reader. It divides the book into historical segments and avoids a verse-by-verse commentary. Though I trust it rests on sound exegesis, its purpose is expository and is designed for inspiration and edification as well as information and enlightenment.

The Acts of the Apostles has been a favorite of mine as far back as I can remember. I have read extensively about it over a long period of years. Therefore, I have not felt constrained to do special research in preparation for this book but have written it more as a reflection of one church historian on the apostolic age based on a long career of teaching and preaching.

One recent book I have found to be unusually helpful from an historical and geographical viewpoint. That is I. Howard Marshall's *The Acts of the Apostles* in the Tyndale New Testament Commentaries, 1980. I have used the distances he has given between places in the course of Paul's travels, though I have tried to check them on maps of the New Testament world.

I agree with Marshall's conservative attitude on most all the historical problems in Acts. I must express perhaps a greater indebtedness in the writing of this book to Ernst Haenchen, the German New Testament scholar, for his book, *The Acts of the Apostles: A Commentary,* Westminster, 1971. This indebtedness, however, is for an entirely different reason. Haenchen gave me a foil for my work. His book, in my opinion, is an example of historical imagination run wild. He transforms the book of Acts into fiction and changes Luke from an historian into a novelist. But perhaps we learn most from those with whom we disagree. The best all-around modern commentary on Acts is still F. F. Bruce's, *The Book of Acts* in the New London Commentary, 1954.

The older works for me are still the best. John Wesley's various comments on Acts in his *Explanatory Notes on the New Testament* are poignant and relevant. *The Life and Epistles of St. Paul* by W. J. Conybeare and J. S. Howson is a literary classic and the best book on Paul I have ever read. Sir William Mitchell Ramsay's *St. Paul the Traveller and the Roman Citizen* was my daily companion on all my Pauline travels, though Ramsay travelled in the nineteenth century and published his book in 1896.

I have visited every place Paul went that is mentioned in the New Testament and have been to all the cities and sites of the Acts of the Apostles. These travels of mine are described in my book, *Journeys after Saint Paul,* MacMillan, 1963.

I am grateful to my pupil, John Beyers, for typing the manuscript and preparing it for the printer, and for all the help given me by The Upper Room in its publication. I am especially grateful to Janice Grana for suggesting that I write the book and to Jill S. Reddig, Douglas Tonks, and their editorial staff for bringing it to successful issue.

INTRODUCTION

LUKE WAS THE first person to write the history of the beginnings of organized Christianity. He composed the Acts of the Apostles before the close of the first century, when all the events he describes took place. No one else attempted to do what he did until the fourth century. As an historian, he is unique among all the writers of the New Testament.

The Acts of the Apostles gives us a chronological account of the development of Christianity from the resurrection and ascension of Jesus to the arrival of Paul in Rome. Why the account stops where it does, no one knows. It could be that Luke wrote the Acts while Paul was still alive and thus was able to solicit the apostle's advice about and criticism of his manuscript. If this were the case, then Acts has to end where it does, for it would have taken the two years that Paul stayed in his own house in Rome for these transactions to take place (Acts 28:30). But this is not likely. There are enough differences between Luke's understanding of Paul's position on certain matters and the apostle's explanation of them to make us doubt that Paul ever saw Luke's manuscript or had anything to do with its composition.

Perhaps Acts ends where it does because the rest of Paul's career was spent in Rome and was so well known to the gentile Christians that anything else said about it would have been redundant. But, then, there were Paul's converts in all the other cities where he had preached throughout the empire. How could they be expected to know the details of his stay in Rome and his execution? The most obvious answer would be that Luke did not know these facts and that he had to stop writing when his information ran out. But this cannot be a satisfactory explanation either, for we know from Paul himself that Luke was still with him in Rome when he wrote his last Epistle just before the end of Nero's reign (2 Tim. 4:11). In all probability, Luke witnessed Paul's execution.

We must admit that it is not now possible to say why Acts ends where it does. It covers a span of more than thirty years and provides us with a thorough knowledge of the origin of Christianity. That is all we have a right to expect of it.

As early as the nineteenth century, German scholars of the Tübingen School accused Luke of an ulterior motive in writing Acts. That motive was to present to posterity a harmonious and unified picture of Christianity by playing down all controversies and differences of opinion, especially those between Peter and Paul, the one the protagonist of Judaism and the other the champion of the rights of the gentiles. This school of thought contended that Acts is an unreliable account of New Testament Christianity, that Luke picks and chooses events at will, that he conceals more than he discloses, so that the picture he gives us of what happened is truncated, partial, incomplete, and even distorted.

If this were the case, it would be reasonable to expect Luke to promote the interests of Paul over those of Peter and to support the gentiles against the Jews. After all, Luke was a gentile, he was the companion and friend of Paul, and he wrote to commend Christianity to the Greeks and Romans. But in the few places we are able to detect differences between what is said in Acts and in other books of the New Testament, those dissimilarities are between Luke and Paul. There are some apparent differences between Acts and the Gospels as well, but none have come to light between Luke and Peter. Maybe the Tübingen School thought Luke toned down Paul to placate Peter. More likely than not, however, the slight differences we find between Luke and Paul in their accounts of the same events are due to ignorance on Luke's part, his lack of knowledge of the intricacies of Jewish law and custom, and his failure to comprehend nuances in Paul's theological interpretations. After all, Luke was a physician, not a theologian.

The reality of the situation is that the Tübingen School had no other comprehensive historical document to set against Acts. All its scholars could do was take bits and pieces of information scattered about in the Pauline Epistles to support their contention. If we are to have any comprehensive chronicle of the early history of Christianity, we have to take Luke's account and treat it reliably, for that is the only one there is.

To be sure, we can scrutinize it at points where it collides with passages in Paul's Epistles; we can take its readings in conjunction with readings from the Gospels when they overlap; and we can collate and also criticize in an effort to understand and evaluate. When we do this, I am persuaded that it is possible to harmonize one passage of scripture with another when we really try. The Acts will stand up favorably with any other historical document from antiquity. It is much safer to accept and use its contents historically and to rely on its author than it is to substitute the speculative opinions and imaginary findings of academicians. Facts are more reliable than hypotheses.

Luke is an historian, but he is an evangelist as well. Where Peter and Paul evangelize by preaching and itinerating as they proclaim the gospel throughout the Roman Empire, Luke evangelizes through his writing, for he believes that one of the best ways to disseminate the gospel and expand the church is to tell the story of how Christianity got started and the heroism and devotion that have characterized its progress thus far. The Gospels tell the matchless story of Jesus. The Acts of the Apostles recounts the inspiring deeds of his apostles. The Holy Spirit is the protagonist of the book of Acts just as Jesus is the protagonist of the Gospels, for the Holy Spirit enables the apostles to do all that they do in the name of Christ. The Acts of the Apostles could just as well be called the Gospel of the Holy Spirit. The Holy Spirit is referred to almost fifty times in Acts, much more than in any other book in the Bible. Luke is the "Father of Christian History and the Evangelist of the Holy Spirit."

CHAPTER ONE

THE RISEN CHRIST AND HIS DISCIPLES

Acts 1:1–26

THE GOSPEL OF LUKE and the Acts of the Apostles, though distinct from each other both in the time of their composition and in their theme and literary design, are nonetheless two volumes of a single work. They were written by the same person whose purpose was to describe the origin and development of Christianity. Therefore, in this first chapter of Acts the author makes the transition from his Gospel of the person and work of Jesus Christ during his ministry in the flesh to the effects of that ministry in the organization of the church.

The connecting link between the two accounts is the risen Christ himself and his postresurrection associations with his disciples. These eventuate in the disciples' first gathering after his ascension and what they do without him to perpetuate his work.

Inscription (1:1)

Luke opens the Acts by addressing it to Theophilus, the same person to whom he had addressed his Gospel (Luke 1:1–4), indicating that he had written both books especially for him. Thus, Theophilus had more of the sacred writings of the New Testament written for and sent to him than any other person or even collection of persons, including the people and churches to whom Paul addressed his Epistles. This is because Luke and Acts, taken together, form a larger literary collection than either the Pauline or the Johannine writings. Luke wrote more of the New Testament than any other author.

However, we know almost nothing about Theophilus. We do not know what he did or where he lived. We are not even sure that he was a baptized Christian. It is reasonable to assume that he was and that the writings were sent to him for his edification. Or he may have been seriously considering becoming a Christian and what Luke sent him was for his instruction before making his decision. He had to have more than a casual interest in the subject to be willing to read so much.

No doubt he was some prominent person who was (or could be) immeasurably influential in the spread of the gospel, and Luke wanted his commendation of his book. Literary works in all periods of history have been dedicated to such persons in order to use their names to promote the dissemination of the writings and more frequently than not to solicit their financial backing as well. The latter was hardly Luke's concern, but the former may have been foremost in his thinking.

Theophilus's name would indicate that he was Greek rather than Latin, but that would not have precluded Roman citizenship and wealth and influence in the empire. The word *theophilus* means "dear to God." Could it be that it was a nickname, indicating the recognition by those who knew him of his devotion to God? It was not unusual in antiquity for this to happen. In the Old Testament, for example, God changed the name of Abram to Abraham to indicate that he was to be the father of many nations (Gen. 17:5) and Jacob to Israel, for he was to rule over a nation in the process of formation even as God rules (Gen. 32:28). In the New Testament, Jesus changed the name of Simon, son of Jonah, to Peter, indicating that he and his faith were the rock on which the church would be built (Matt. 16:17–18). Saul of Tarsus, after he was converted, changed his Jewish name to its Latin equivalent, Paul, to signify that his mission was to the gentiles.

That is why some scholars have felt that Luke's Theophilus was not an historical personage at all. They assume the name in Acts is a pseudonym for a collective personality, a community of many people, perhaps even the entire Christian church of the first century. Though this explanation of Luke's inscription and greeting is dubious and Theophilus was probably a real person, this is a poignant idea. As a matter of fact, the Acts of the Apostles has come to belong to all persons in all ages who think of themselves as dear to God and who have been blessed by this book.

Christ's Departing Charge to His Disciples (1:2–8)

Luke refers to his Gospel when he mentions that the risen Christ had demonstrated that he was alive after his crucifixion by many indisputable signs. He does not identify these signs because Theophilus and those who had read his Gospel already knew what they were.

Luke uses the word *passion* in referring to the death of Jesus (1:3). By doing that, he emphasizes, without describing the horror of our Lord's execution, the shame and mistreatment to which he was subjected during the course of his trial: the crown of thorns pressed on his head and the scourging, the pain of which was so excruciating that many did not survive it. This is the only time the word *passion* in this sense appears in the entire Bible.

Today, we generally use the word as a synonym for *lust* or *sexual desire* to mean "intense emotion, excitement, strong feeling, and ardent affection." But by his limiting the word to convey intense suffering, Luke introduces the term into the Christian vocabulary. Occasionally in Christian history it describes the suffering and death of martyrs, but almost always *passion* refers to the sufferings of Christ between the Last Supper and his death on the cross.

From the Acts, we learn the length of time Christ spent on earth between his resurrection and ascension. In reading Luke's Gospel, one gets the impression that all the post-resurrection appearances took place on Easter Day, that Christ arose from the dead in the early morning and ascended into heaven in the late afternoon. But Luke in Acts states that Christ was seen by his disciples over a period of forty days (1:3), during which time he taught them about the kingdom of God. Christ was concerned not with the church as we know it in the form of a temporal organization, but with the reign of God both in heaven and on earth. That reign can and does express itself in and through the church when the church is obedient to the will of God as Christ himself has defined it.

We have difficulty comprehending this distinction, however. In our thought and activity we tend to concentrate on the organization we call the church, and we constantly substitute it for the kingdom of God. Our actions show that we think it is the kingdom of God on earth.

We come by this impression honestly, for that was precisely what the disciples thought, too. Since Jesus was alive and had conquered death, they fully expected him to restore the kingdom of Israel, and they asked him when he planned to do it (1:6). "Can we expect it right now?" they asked. "Only God the Father has the answer to that question," Jesus replied.

His plans for them were of an entirely different order. Their sole mission on this earth was to witness to him (1:8). But they would have to wait to accomplish the assignment until God endowed them with the power, which would come through the baptism of the Holy Spirit.

Jesus reminded them that John the Baptist had baptized only with water. To understand the full import of baptism by the Holy Spirit, they should think of it in terms of the method John used in baptizing his followers. He either immersed them or poured water over them so that they were totally covered with water. In the same way the Holy Spirit would engulf them. They would be deluged in the Spirit's grace. His power would be infused throughout their whole personality. That, Jesus reminded them, was the promise God had given them through him.

He told them that their empowering would take place shortly in Jerusalem. Because Jerusalem was the place of his humiliation and death, it is only appropriate that it should have been the place of his vindication as the Holy Spirit began to work through his disciples.

In that mood, and in that setting, Jesus issued his final commandment to his disciples; that commandment is known as their commission. After they received the Holy Spirit, they were to witness to Christ, first in Jerusalem and Judea, then in Samaria, and finally "unto the uttermost part of the earth" (1:8). That meant their proclamation of the gospel must begin at home. Then, they must carry it to their enemies. Finally, they must extend their work of evangelization all over the world.

The Ascension (1:9–11)

While the disciples watched him, Jesus was taken from them and passed through a thick cloud into heaven. They were still gazing up into the sky when two angels reminded them that they had work to do on earth. The angels assured them that the way Jesus went up into heaven would be the same way he would come back again from heaven. He had promised that if he went away from them, he would come again to them (John 14:18; 16:16).

Luke devotes only three verses to the ascension. We are not to conclude, however, that the event was unimportant to him. After he said what happened and how it happened, there was nothing more to add to his account. The ascension proved to be most significant to the early church. The oldest creed, the Apostles' Creed, carries it as one of the articles of faith, the belief in which is essential to becoming a Christian.

The ascension is the basis of our understanding of the parousia. In his first advent, Jesus was born, like everyone else, of a woman. Though his preexistent life had been in heaven, he emptied himself of his heavenly glory, gave up his divine status, and became a human being, just another man (Phil. 2:6–8). But when he comes the second time, he will descend from the clouds of heaven in majesty and glory to judge the living and the dead. Every knee shall bow before him, and every tongue shall confess him as Lord (Phil. 2:10–11).

There is nothing we can do or fail to do to prevent this from happening. Even if we destroy all life on this earth through nuclear explosions, we cannot interfere with our Lord's second coming. Nothing can possibly separate Christ from his own, "neither death, nor life, nor angels, nor principalities, nor powers, nor things present, nor things to come, nor height, nor depth, nor any other creature" (Rom. 8:38–39). The second coming of Christ will not be a gradual process but will be a cataclysmic event. According to Acts, it will be the exact reversal of his ascension.

The Apostolate (1:12–26)

A disciple was any follower of Jesus. The Twelve were disciples, but of a special class. They were Jesus' intimates, his closest and dearest friends. After his ascension, the disciples who remained loyal to Jesus would become apostles, the nucleus of the church, its supreme pastors and shepherds, its constituted leadership. Their names are listed in this passage of Acts (1:13), the same list, with the exception of Judas, that Luke gives in his Gospel (Luke 6:14–16).

Other followers (disciples) gathered with them at a designated place in Jerusalem. According to tradition, it was where the Last Supper had been held, the house of the mother of John Mark and the sister of Barnabas. Among those present were the mother of Jesus and his brothers and also some women, probably Mary Magdalene and the others who had helped prepare Jesus' body for burial. This means that women participated along with the men in the very first conclave of Christendom. There were approximately 120 persons, perhaps that many men. According to Jewish law, 120 men was the minimum number necessary to organize a new community with its own governing council.

Peter took charge of the group. He addressed the little assembly and said that a successor to Judas had to be designated. Judas was the guide of the high priest's soldiers when they arrested Jesus in the Garden of Gethsemane. Peter affirmed that Jesus' betrayal by Judas was prophesied by David in the Psalms when he wrote, "Yea, mine own familiar friend, in whom I trusted, which did eat of my bread, hath lifted up his heel against me" (Psalm 41:9). The field Judas bought with the reward the chief priests gave him for betraying Jesus was uninhabitable, and David foresaw this as well (Psalm 69:25). David by prophecy instructs us, said Peter, to fill Judas's vacant office (Psalm 109:8).

At this time the disciples hoped to convert their fellow countrymen to faith in Jesus. They remembered Jesus' promise to them that they would sit on thrones and judge the twelve tribes of Israel (Luke 22:30). They no doubt had this in mind when they asked Jesus if he was about to restore the kingdom to Israel. Whenever the promise was fulfilled, there must be twelve persons among them to rule; Judas had to be replaced.

In his speech Peter recounts the manner of Judas's death. He says Judas fell headlong on the ground in the field he had purchased with his reward and ruptured himself so that his bowels spilled out of his body. Matthew gives a different account in his Gospel; he states that Judas in shame returned the money to the chief priests and went out and hanged himself (Matt. 27:3–5).

Although these two accounts seem to contradict each other, both could be correct. Judas may well have hanged himself, and his body could have hung on the tree undiscovered until it began to rot. Then as it was cut down in such a decayed condition, it could have fallen apart on impact with the ground. The priests could have used Judas's money to buy the potter's field in which to bury strangers (Matt. 27:7), and by their doing so, Judas in effect purchased the field by proxy.

Peter addresses the group with the words, "Men and brethren" (1:16). This is the first time in scripture "brethren" (brothers) is used to designate Christians.

The conditions imposed on any person selected to take the place of Judas were that he had been a disciple and had kept company with Jesus and the eleven from the baptism by John until the ascension. He had to be a witness with them of all that Jesus had said and done during his earthly ministry. The company selected two persons who met those qualifications: Joseph called Barsabas, whose Latin name was Justus, and Matthias. They turned the men over to the Lord, who alone knows the hearts of all people, and asked the Lord to make the final choice. They expected God to do this through their casting of lots. So after they had prayed, they cast lots, and the lot favored Matthias, who then took his place with the eleven.

On the basis of this procedure, scholars have contended that the supreme leadership of the first church was not elected but was divinely selected and appointed. This is certainly true of the eleven, for Jesus himself chose all of them, but that claim is questionable in regard to Matthias. Maybe God did make the final choice—if we can bring ourselves to consider the casting of lots a legitimate way of ascertaining the divine mind. But the company gave God only two possibilities from which to make a choice. This procedure hardly commends itself as proof of the establishment of a divinely called ministry. The brethren made sure that God would not put someone over them that they did not want. We do not hear any more about Matthias. Maybe God did not make a choice at that time after all. Perhaps God decided to postpone making a choice until a later time when Saul of Tarsus could be appointed.

The eleven disciples and Matthias became apostles during this assembly. The apostles were to witness to the resurrection of Jesus and, in so doing, win others to the Christian cause by enabling them to confess their faith in Jesus Christ.

CHAPTER TWO

THE BIRTH OF THE CHURCH

Acts 2:1–47

JESUS DID NOT establish the church. To be sure, he was the originating cause of the church; that is to say, that without his life, his ministry, his teaching, and his death and resurrection, there would have been no church. But he did not actually organize it. He did not personally frame its polity or constitute its discipline. Jesus was the impetus given to the apostles to establish the church. He was the inspiration and stimulus for organized Christianity. He anticipated the institution founded by those who came after him and to which they gave his name.

The nature of the church is so different from the nature of any other social institution that it is hardly correct to think of it as having been established by any person or collection of persons, even the apostles themselves. The best way to picture the origin of the Christian church is in terms of birth. Maybe it is providential that Luke's placement for the beginning of the church in the book of Acts falls at exactly the same place as his description of the birth of Jesus in his Gospel—in the second chapter. The church is the extension in time of the incarnation. It is the continuation in corporate form of Christ's personal presence. Indeed, it is the body of Christ. It is the historical institutionalization of Christ's ministry and the life-giving properties of his death and resurrection.

The Holy Spirit is the founder of the church. Just as

Jesus was conceived by the Holy Spirit to be born of the Virgin Mary, even so the church was given its corporate life by that same Spirit. As God once lived on earth as a human being in the Second Person of the Trinity, so God resides now in the Third Person of the Trinity in the church and in its members. The Holy Spirit is God still living among and in God's people. Thus, it is correct to say that at a given time in history the Christian church was born of the Holy Spirit.

Pentecost (2:1)

This birth of the church by the Holy Spirit took place on the day of Pentecost. Next to Christmas and Easter, Pentecost is the greatest day in the Christian year. On that day the paraments on the altars of our churches are red, and the ministers wear red stoles over their shoulders. Red is the liturgical color for the Season after Pentecost, which can extend now from Pentecost Sunday until the beginning of Advent. Trinity Sunday follows Pentecost, and some churches begin Trinity Season on that day, which limits the Season of Pentecost to only one week. United Methodists renamed Trinity Season Kingdomtide. But no matter how we divide the Christian calendar into seasons, Pentecost itself is one of the three great feast days of the Christian year. Since Christmas seldom falls on Sunday, Pentecost Sunday is second only to Easter as the most important Sunday in the Christian year.

Yet the word *Pentecost* occurs in the Bible only three times, all in the New Testament (Acts 2:1, 20:16; 1 Cor. 16:8). The latter two refer to Paul; in the first instance, it is indicated that he has to be in Jerusalem at Pentecost, and on the second occasion, he says he will remain in Ephesus until Pentecost.

Pentecost means "fiftieth day." It corresponds to the Jewish Feast of Weeks, which was a one-day religious observance that came fifty days after Passover. On that day the first fruits of the wheat and corn harvest were presented to the Lord God in the Temple. All Old Testament holy days commemorate some special event in Israelite history, and the Feast of Weeks is no exception. It recalls God's covenant with Noah and later with Moses. It came to be the anniversary of the promulgation of the law by God from Mount Sinai through Moses. There is a rabbinical tradition that the Ten Commandments were issued by God in the several languages of the seventy nations of antiquity.

Pentecost comes fifty days after Easter Day. The Passover is the anniversary of the deliverance of the Hebrew people from Egyptian slavery, and the Feast of Weeks is the anniversary of God's constitution for the establishment of a new nation. Without the law, the state of Israel in the Promised Land could never have come into existence. Likewise, Easter, as the anniversary of the resurrection, is the celebration of Christ's conquest of death and his victory over the grave. Pentecost, then, signalizes the gift of the power of the resurrection to Christ's followers and the constitution of a new Israel—the church—to supersede the old Israel.

Before that could happen, however, two requirements had to be met. The first was that the people who would constitute the new Israel, that is, the first members of this emerging organization, the original corporate manifestation of the body of Christ, had to be of "one accord." They had to possess a single mind. They had to share the same ideal. Divisiveness among them would have meant ruin for the whole enterprise and would have thwarted the plan of almighty God.

The Christian church could never have been born had Judas Iscariot remained in the lot. He would have polarized the group and prevented the unity necessary for the accomplishment of God's purpose. But his contrary attitudes and actions seem to have died with him. Fortunately, there was no other "Judas" in that illustrious company on that first Christian Pentecost.

The second requirement that had to be met was that the people had to be gathered together in one place. They could not be scattered abroad. When the glorious transaction took place, they all had to participate in it.

From its very inception, Christianity has been a social movement. The plan of what it should be and the motivation for it did not come to just one individual who had to convince others of the value of what he recommended. In this regard it was entirely different from Buddhism, Confucianism, and Islam. The church was born through a collection of people who were assembled together in one place. It did not originate under a Bo tree or in a scholar's study or on the sands of the desert. It began in an upper room.

Empowerment by the Holy Spirit (2:2–13)

Under such circumstances, the Holy Spirit came and transformed that small collection of people into the first congregation of the Christian church. Luke uses two symbols—wind and fire—to describe the descent of the Spirit; a symbol is a sign, an indication, not the reality itself. He says that those present heard a sound out of heaven like a strong, swift wind blowing through the whole house. At the same time they saw above them streaks of bright light like fire. Evidently their vision was that of bolts of lightning striking all about them. The Holy Spirit was manifested to them by both what they heard and what they saw. Pentecost for those first followers of Jesus was an audiovisual experience.

According to the account, however, the sound was more than mere sound. It became almost tangible to them. Indeed, the noise that sounded like wind whistling in the distance proved to be wind and blew in on them so that they felt what they heard. The blowing, whistling wind illustrates the pervasiveness of the Holy Spirit, which reached and affected everyone in that first Christian congregation.

There is no Old Testament equivalent for this. God was not in the wind that blew in the face of Elijah as he stood waiting for God atop Mount Horeb in the wilderness (1 Kings 19:11). However, Jesus used the image of wind to explain to Nicodemus the coming and going of the Spirit, whose presence one always feels when one experiences the new birth, is "born again," so to speak, in the image of God, and becomes an entirely new person (John 3:8). That is precisely what happened to those people on the day of Pentecost.

The symbol of fire for the Holy Spirit does have its equivalent in the Old Testament. God led the people out of Egypt by a pillar of cloud by day and a pillar of fire by night (Exod. 13:21). Fire illustrates the guidance the Holy Spirit will give the followers of Jesus as they undertake their mission in the world. He will show them what to do and how to do it. He will enable them to convict people of sin, to warn them of God's judgment, and to make them righteous (John 16:8). In other words, the same thing the Spirit has done for them at Pentecost, he will through their agency do for all those who believe and accept the gospel they proclaim.

Luke says that the bright light that looked like fire settled on each one of them; that is, a separate tongue of fire lapped every person—a bolt of lightning struck each and every individual. At Pentecost those people were set on fire spiritually by the Holy Spirit. They gained divine energy; they no longer operated as mere human beings. Their strength and influence were the strength and influence of almighty God. When Luke says that they were all filled with the Holy Spirit, he means that their personalities no longer belonged to them but belonged to God. It was no longer they who lived but Christ by the Holy Spirit who lived in them (Gal. 2:20).

The immediate result of the descent of the Holy Spirit on that little congregation at Pentecost was the ability the Spirit gave some of them to speak in languages other than their own. The languages were not unknown tongues in the sense of being something different from any languages spoken by people on earth. What each spoke was unknown to him before he spoke it, but it was not unknown to those to whom it was spoken. And evidently each person spoke a different language from every other person; there was a variety in communication corresponding to all the languages that the foreigners in Jerusalem understood. The purpose of speaking in other tongues was not for the personal edification of the Christians but simply as means of converting unbelievers. This gift, therefore, was altogether utilitarian.

The response of those who heard, as might have been expected, was mixed. Some were most favorably impressed and wanted to hear more and ponder the meaning of what they heard relative to their own life and destiny. Others discredited what the followers of Jesus said, made fun of them, and claimed that they must be drunk to make such extravagant claims for this new faith and for their risen Lord. But, no matter, both those that took them seriously and those that did not were equally amazed and perplexed to hear the presumably ignorant Galileans conversing fluently with them in their own languages.

Luke is very careful to enumerate the countries from which all the people came. They were all Jews of the Dispersion. There was a larger population of Jews scattered throughout the Roman Empire and its borders than lived in Jerusalem itself, almost as many as lived in the whole of Judea and Galilee and the other territories that constituted the old kingdom of Israel. The Jews of the Dispersion tried at least once in their lifetime to attend one of the feasts in Jerusalem. Of course most tried to be there at Passover. Wealthy Jews from abroad came often on such occasions to Jerusalem, and it was not unusual for them to move to the Holy City in their old age in order to die and be buried in the land of their forefathers, the land of Abraham, Isaac, and Jacob.

One might expect such people to know Hebrew, but most of them did not. Practically all of them had forgotten their native tongue. The Old Testament had to be translated into Greek to satisfy the Jewish population in Alexandria, Egypt. Even the inhabitants of the homeland itself had forgotten Hebrew. Jesus and his followers spoke only Aramaic.

The countries Luke names indicate that the people came from all parts of the known world. He wants thereby to show the international character of Christianity from its inception. At the outset, it addressed itself to the whole world, for many of the Jews were proselytes, that is, Judaized Greeks, Romans, and Orientals.

Peter's Proclamation of the Gospel (2:14–36)

The very first act of this newly constituted Christian congregation was to preach the gospel to unbelievers. Evangelization is the soul of Christianity. After the Spirit descended on that little company at Pentecost, its members did not remain in the upper room to sing hymns together, pray for one another, and reenact Jesus' last meal with them by breaking and eating bread and drinking wine together in memory of his death and in anticipation of his second coming. They went immediately into the streets of Jerusalem to witness to others and to announce the good news about Jesus Christ.

The first sermon to be preached by the infant church was delivered by Peter in Jerusalem on the day of Pentecost. Luke is ambivalent as to how many persons the Spirit gave the power to speak in other languages. Probably it was only the twelve apostles, for the other eleven alone stood up with Peter when he preached his sermon. It is obvious from the beginning of the church, when Matthias was chosen to succeed Judas, that there was a duly constituted ministry distinct from the membership at large. The first ministers were the apostles, and their primary responsibility was to preach the gospel.

Peter used the accusation of the mockers in the crowd that the disciples were drunk as the lead-in for his sermon. He said it was too early in the morning for people to start drinking; they had not even eaten breakfast. What the crowd saw in those witnesses was a demonstration of the power of the Holy Spirit prophesied by Joel in the Jewish scripture (Joel 2:28–32). The disciples of Jesus, inspired by the Holy Spirit, had dreamed dreams and seen visions, and they could not help prophesying. Earlier, God had shown wonders in the heavens and signs on the earth. At the death of Jesus, the day had suddenly become night, an earthquake had struck Jerusalem, the veil of the Temple had been rent in twain, and the graves had given up their dead (Matt. 27:51–53).

This Jesus, who had demonstrated that God approved him by miracles and wonders, had been arrested and convicted by the very people to whom Peter preached, and they caused him to be crucified by the Romans. Peter denounced them for this in his sermon, accusing them of killing their own Messiah. But God raised Jesus from the dead, as King David himself had prophesied. What reads like a statement by David about himself (Psalm 16:8–11) Peter interpreted as David's description of what would happen to the Messiah. He told the crowd that David could not have been talking of himself, for David had died and been buried and his tomb was visible to them in Jerusalem.

Jesus of Nazareth was the person whose soul God would not leave among the dead. It was he whom God raised up to sit at God's right hand in glory. It was Jesus the Messiah who had sent the Holy Spirit to empower Peter and the other disciples, and the people were witnessing now in them the demonstrations of the Spirit. The people at large had not witnessed the resurrection. Only the intimate friends and followers of Jesus had seen the tomb immediately after Jesus had vacated it. Only they had had fellowship with him after his resurrection. And they alone had watched him ascend to heaven. But the demonstrations of the Holy Spirit in the words and deeds of the apostles and the other followers of Jesus on the day of Pentecost were public acts that anyone who was present could see and hear.

Peter brought his majestic sermon to a close by proclaiming that the person his auditors had crucified, God had designated as their Lord and their Messiah.

The Response of the People and the Pattern of the Church
(2:37–47)

The people were deeply moved by Peter's sermon. He convinced them of the truth of what he said and also convicted them of their sins. Their response was immediate and positive. They asked Peter and the other apostles what they should do. They wanted to be told how to amend their lives and become acceptable to God. They wanted to know how they could be saved.

The only way, Peter told them, was for them to repent of what they had done and to be baptized in the name of Jesus Christ. Then they would receive a double gift: their sins would be forgiven, and they would also receive the gift of the Holy Spirit. In other words, the new converts could expect the same empowerment by the Holy Spirit that they had witnessed in the words and deeds of the little company in the upper room who had known and loved the Lord when he sojourned with them on earth. These gifts of the Spirit might differ in their various recipients. Certainly the new converts could not expect to be apostles. Nonetheless, they, too, would become effective witnesses to their Lord.

Three thousand people were converted on the day of Pentecost as a result of Peter's sermon. As they took their places as new members of the emerging church, the pattern of organization of the believing community began gradually to take shape. Its form was very simple, but some of its features have remained as characteristics of the body of Christ.

At its heart was the teaching ministry entrusted to the twelve apostles who had been with Jesus, listened to his words, and knew his mind. It is safe to assume that preaching went hand in hand with teaching, both being expressive of the same truth, the teaching designed to nurture and edify the believing flock while the preaching won new converts.

The church was a place of fellowship where members shared a common meal as often as they could and where also, presumably as a part of their worship, they ate bread and drank wine ceremoniously in remembrance of their Lord's death and in anticipation of his coming. Voluntarily they shared what they had with one another, putting their material resources at the disposal of the congregation as needs arose. There is no proof that they lived together in one community as the Essenes did.

They did not break at first with their Jewish past. They still worshiped daily in the Temple, but they also met in one another's homes that they might increase in their understanding of the apostles' doctrine.

As they praised God and as the apostles did many wonderful things, they at first found favor with all the people, and every day new converts were added to the church.

THE CHURCH IN JERUSALEM

Acts 3:1–8:3

JERUSALEM SHOULD BE, and spiritually is, the primatial see of Christendom. In the beginning, the city was where all the action was. The church was born within its walls. Both Easter and Pentecost happened there.

The five chapters of the Acts of the Apostles that follow immediately after Pentecost are confined entirely to work in Jerusalem. And from what they say and what they leave unsaid, it is apparent that initially there was no Christian activity outside Jerusalem. Jesus had told them just before his ascension to witness to him first in that city (1:8), and they heeded our Lord's admonition.

The First Healing Miracle (3:1–11)

It is hardly correct to say that the healing of the lame man at the Temple was the very first miracle that any of the apostles performed after the ascension of Jesus. Their speaking in foreign tongues was a miracle. The conversion of three thousand people as a result of Peter's sermon displayed miraculous power on the part of the preacher. But the healing of this man is the first specific miracle performed by any of the apostles on just one person afflicted with a particular malady apparent to everyone who saw him. The man had been unable to walk since birth; he had to be carried everywhere he went.

Though Luke does record that the disciples were able to heal when Jesus sent them forth on their first mission as emissaries of his kingdom (9:6), this seems to have been a glorious exception. Most of the time during Jesus' ministry, they had been unable to perform miracles. Once, for example, while Jesus was away from them, the disciples had been embarrassed when a father had asked them to heal his epileptic son and they had failed in their attempt to do so (Matt. 17:14–21; Mark 9:14–29; Luke 9:37–43).

When Jesus had told the disciples that those who believed in him would do works such as they had seen him do, and even greater works than he had performed, his words had sounded incredible to them (John 14:12). Yet what he had promised would happen was happening. It was as if Jesus were still with them and responding to the needs of the sick and afflicted people who called on him for help. Indeed, he was present through the activity of the Holy Spirit operating through the works of the apostles.

It was three o'clock in the afternoon when Peter and John, on their way to the Temple to observe the offering of the sacrifice, to join in the prayers of the congregation, and to receive the priestly blessing, were accosted by a lame man asking alms. The man had himself carried each morning to the main entrance to the Temple so that he could beg alms of all who passed through. It was a major expression of Jewish piety to give alms to the poor. Indeed, the Pharisees liked to display their generosity in that fashion. Practically everyone who entered that gate gave alms to as many beggars as happened to be on hand to receive them. Each beggar had his own special spot from which to beg, and such persons often had quite a good income from begging.

Probably the Beautiful Gate was the one inside the Temple connecting the Court of the Gentiles to the Court of the Women, where only Jews were permitted to enter. It was known as the Nicanor Gate and was the site of the heaviest traffic, at least of persons with the greatest motive to give. The gate was made of bronze in Corinthian style and arrested the attention of gentile tourists who could look at it but could not enter it.

Peter and John did not give any money to the lame man who asked alms of them. He was at first very disappointed by their response. Peter addressed him, "I do not have any silver or gold to give you. What I do have, however, is yours, and you can take it right now" (3:6, AP). The poor fellow did not see the two apostles carrying any sacks of fruit or grain. Therefore, if Peter were not going to give him money, what else could he expect but advice? And that was the last thing on earth he wanted. But soon he felt strength in his ankles and legs. Peter took his hand and lifted him up. He began to leap and dance and praise God as he went with Peter and John into the Temple for the afternoon sacrifice and public prayers. He had no petitions to offer; his prayers were all thanks and praise to God.

Explanation and Exhortation (3:12–26)

Many people had seen what had happened, so when Peter, John, and the formerly lame man emerged from the service, quite a crowd had gathered in the Court of the Gentiles and the Colonnade of Solomon on its east side. Peter did not miss the opportunity to explain to the astonished audience what had happened. He began by asking the people why they were all staring at him and John. They were not magicians. It was not by their power or holiness, he said, that they had made the lame man to walk. He was made to walk through faith in the name of Jesus. It was Jesus, and he alone, who had made the man's legs healthy and strong. All Peter and John had done was to exercise on this lame man their faith in the all-powerful name of Jesus. And now the man on whom the miracle had been performed had faith, too. He had lost his business as a professional beggar, but he was glad to lose it in order to become a whole person and begin a new life as a disciple of Jesus Christ.

In this miracle, Peter told the crowd, you have seen how the God of your fathers has glorified Jesus, the very person you arrested and accused before Pontius Pilate and had executed. Though Jesus was holy and just, you chose a murderer in his place when Pilate offered to release him and set him free. With those words, Peter had given a complete explanation of the event.

But Peter was too skillful an evangelist to stop with an explanation of what had happened. He wanted to make an application of what he said to the needs of the people and evoke a response from them. He perceived their interest and concern. He did not want to leave them with a sense of helplessness and desperation over the evil they had inflicted on Jesus.

Immediately he turned from condemnation to hope and assurance by telling them that he knew, and God knew, that what they and their rulers had done was done out of ignorance. For that reason God would forgive them if they would repent and be converted. "In the plan of God," Peter exclaimed, "Jesus had to suffer and die. However, the person you killed is not dead. God raised him from the dead and heaven has received him, where he will remain until the time when God shall send him back again to restore all things to their original state. This has been predicted by all the prophets, who have assured you that you are the people of the covenant to whom God sent Jesus." That was the time for them to take advantage of God's gift to them by turning away from their sins and acknowledging Jesus.

In Peter's brief exhortation some theological implications should arrest our attention as evidence of what had already become the convictions of the apostles and were through their teachings to become guiding principles in the life of the primitive church. Peter called Jesus "the Holy One and the Just" (3:14), ascribing attributes to him that belong only to God. To be sure, Elisha had been called "a holy man of God" (2 Kings 4:9) and Aaron "the saint of the Lord" (Psalm 106:16), but in both instances the possessive preposition follows the adjectival phrase or noun, indicating the derivative nature of the appellation. But the title Peter gave Jesus was without modification and was synonymous with what the Jews to whom he spoke gave to God.

He likewise called Jesus "the Prince of life" (3:15), indicating that he whom God raised from the dead has God's power to confer life on all who believe. The decision of life and death to all people is in his hands, for Moses foretold that another prophet like him would arise (Deut. 18:15, 19) whom the people must hear or else be destroyed. When Samuel took the kingdom from Saul and gave it to David, he must have known that the ultimate fulfillment of that kingdom had to be through Jesus Christ.

If Luke is faithfully recording Peter's thoughts about Jesus, and there is no reason to think that he is not, then this is the oldest expression of Christology in the New Testament, and it places Jesus Christ the Son on a parity with God the Father. Peter's testimony was given while Saul of Tarsus was still an unbeliever and many years before the Apostle John composed his Gospel and Epistles.

The Action of the Sanhedrin and the Reaction of the Church (4:1–5:16)

Peter and John were arrested because Peter had evoked the name of Jesus as the cause of the miracle he had performed. The rulers of the Jews had had enough trouble with Jesus while he was alive on earth. They could not afford the continuance of his influence through the demagoguery of his disciples. The captain of the Temple, who was next in prestige and power to the high priest, accompanied by some of the priests and a group of Sadducees, put the two apostles in custody. They were offended because Peter and John taught through the power of Jesus the resurrection from the dead. The Sadducees did not believe in a resurrection. Whereas the Pharisees instigated the opposition to Jesus, the Sadducees sought to curtail the activities of the infant church. The most powerful faction in the Sanhedrin, they composed the majority of the elders in that group.

Peter and John were kept under guard overnight near the Temple precincts, and the next day they were arraigned before the Sanhedrin. Luke lists Annas as the high priest at this time and Caiaphas, John, and Alexander along with him. In fact, Annas had been deposed as high priest by the Romans in about A.D. 14, and Caiaphas was still in office. Caiaphas was Annas's son-in-law, and John, or Jonathan, and Alexander were Annas's sons. Most of the high priests who succeeded Annas were of his family; though not high priest in name, he retained the influence and power. He continued to make the decisions as he had during the trial of Jesus. Peter pointed to the man who had been lame all his life and said to the Sanhedrin, "It is because of Jesus, whom you crucified but whom God raised from the dead, that this man stands before you hardy and well" (4:10, AP).

Two facts stand out in this trial. First, the members of the Sanhedrin did not dispute the miracle of the healing of the lame man. They could not, for there he was standing before them on his own two feet, which he had never been able to do before. Second, they did not deny the resurrection of Jesus from the dead. By then, the event must have been widely accepted throughout Jerusalem.

Peter accosted his judges by defiantly asserting that there is no other name but Jesus given among them whereby they can be saved. In other words, their religion is inadequate. Like everyone else, they must accept Jesus if they expect to be saved. After consultation among themselves, the members of the Sanhedrin ordered Peter and John to desist from preaching in the name of Jesus and threatened them if they continued to extol him. But the two men defiantly responded by asking them whether it was better to obey them or God, insisting that they were compelled by God to speak about the things they had seen and heard.

Despite the apostles' defiant attitude, the Sanhedrin let them go. Some scholars think that a Jewish law compelled the Sanhedrin to treat a first offense with a simple warning in case the offender was ignorant of the law he had broken. But Luke says the Sanhedrin could not afford to expose itself to the wrath of the people. Five thousand people had been converted as a result of Peter's sermon following the miracle. Those people were all in and about the Temple precincts, and they knew that Peter and John were on trial inside the hall of the Sanhedrin.

When Peter and John were released, they went immediately to the Christian congregation to give a report, and they inspired the group with their courage and boldness. The resurrection proved that Jesus could not be subdued by his enemies, and that same power through the Holy Spirit was now given to them.

The prayer the congregation prayed when Peter and John returned ended in the petition that all of them be given boldness to speak God's word and demonstrate God's power through healing and other signs and wonders, all to be done in the precious name of Jesus. At the end of the prayer, the place where they met was shaken as by an earthquake, and they received what they prayed for. Luke tells us that they were filled with the Holy Spirit and they spoke God's word with boldness. This was a second Pentecost. New converts were given what the original disciples had received on the day of Pentecost—the gift of the Holy Spirit. Luke calls the congregation a multitude; since three thousand had been converted at Pentecost and five thousand more as a result of the healing of the lame man, the number of Christians in Jerusalem comprised a noticeable portion of the population.

Nonetheless, Luke indicates two amazing characteristics of their life together. One is that they were free of factions. Their unity in Christ was so complete that they were animated by a single purpose: "And the multitude of them that believed were of one heart and of one soul" (4:32). The other is that none of them considered his or her property as anything more than a material means of helping others. They pooled their resources and as a community held all things in common. Therefore, no one in the Christian community lacked anything because each person received according to individual needs. The Christians entrusted their goods to the twelve apostles, and the apostles decided the extent of each person's needs and made the necessary appropriations. When people sold their properties, they immediately brought the proceeds from the sale and in an act of worship laid them at the apostles' feet.

Luke cites Joses, nicknamed Barnabas by the apostles because of his ability to console individuals, as an example of this practice. He sold land and gave the money from the sale to the apostles. Barnabas was a Cypriot Jew who had holdings in Jerusalem. He was the uncle of Mark, being the brother of Mark's mother (Col. 4:10). Luke adds that he was a Levite, which means that he was a descendant of Moses and Aaron with traditional connections with the Temple, though he belonged to the Dispersion and came only occasionally to Jerusalem.

The surrender of one's wealth to the apostles was not a requirement of the Christian community; it was entirely voluntary. A married couple named Ananias and Sapphira, who were already members of the community but still held on to their possessions, decided to sell a piece of property and give some of the proceeds to the apostles. However, they pretended to give the entire amount. They wanted full credit for only a partial contribution. Ananias made the gift, but instead of receiving praise from Peter for his generosity, he was condemned for lying.

The apostle accused him of two things: first, yielding to Satan, who put the evil thought in his mind; and second, lying to the Holy Spirit. This double accusation is of great importance in our understanding of the incident. Jesus had said that the one unforgivable sin is sin against the Holy Spirit (Matt. 12:31; Mark 3:29). The Pharisees, for example, had attributed the mighty works of Christ to the devil (Matt. 9:33–34). Persons who attribute the acts of God to the devil cannot hope to be saved because they are incapable of distinguishing between good and evil and thwart the overtures of the Holy Spirit toward them at every turn. This is what Peter discerned in Ananias. He had put his own interests before those of God and the Christian community, had yielded to the devil, and as a result had lied to the Holy Spirit. When Peter told him what he had done, he fell over dead.

Three hours later Sapphira arrived, not knowing what had happened to her husband. Peter gave her the opportunity to correct the mistake by telling the truth, but she repeated the same lie that Ananias had told, and she suffered the same fate. It is dangerous to lie. It is fatal to lie to the Holy Spirit.

In connection with this lugubrious incident Luke uses the word *church* for the second time in Acts. He uses it first when we would expect him to use it—immediately after Pentecost, when he says that "the Lord added to the church daily such as should be saved" (2:47). But here he says, in contrast to the joy and praise that marked the church after Pentecost and the favor it enjoyed with all the people, that "great fear came upon all the church, and upon as many as heard these things" (5:11). To be sure, the church is primarily a joyous fellowship where people find their unity and strength in love and devotion to Jesus Christ. But the church is also God's house of judgment, where God's prophetic word discerns and condemns evil and where unrepentant sinners are brought down.

The apostles continued to work wonders, proclaim the gospel, and make their presence known on Solomon's Porch within the walls of the Temple precinct. People came from outside Jerusalem to hear them and to have their sick cured. The lame and diseased were laid on pallets in the streets so that the shadow of Peter in passing by might fall on them and work a miraculous cure. Multitudes, says Luke, were added to the Christian body.

Persecution, Dissension, and Martyrdom (5:17–8:3)

The gains the Christians were making were too great for the Jewish authorities to tolerate. Jerusalem was a relatively small city, estimated by some to have had no more than twenty-five thousand inhabitants. During celebrations it may have swelled to as many as one hundred thousand. Of course its population was swollen by pilgrims and tourists at the times of the religious feasts. Through the apostles' efforts, natives and visitors alike were being converted. It is reasonable to suppose that the church now had between twelve and fifteen thousand members, and it was continuing to gain at every turn.

Consequently, the high priest and the dominant Sadducean party in the Sanhedrin incarcerated all the apostles. When the Sanhedrin met and the apostles were sent for to be tried, they could not be found in the prison. The angel of the Lord had intervened and set them free. They were right back where they were when they had been arrested, in the very Temple itself, teaching the people. They were brought in without resistance to the Sanhedrin, and the high priest indignantly accused them of doing precisely what he had commanded them not to do, that is, teaching "in this name." He deliberately did not add "Jesus." He would not condescend to utter the name of that malefactor. He did say, however, that it was the purpose of the apostles to bring "this man's blood upon" them.

But what else could they expect? Had they not said to Pilate, when he washed his hands of the guilt of condemning Jesus, "His blood be on us, and on our children" (Matt. 27:24)? That is exactly what the apostles reminded them of, as they said through Peter, "We ought to obey God rather than men" (5:29). Peter also stated that Jesus, whom they killed, God has exalted and made to be a Prince and a Savior in order to bring Israel to repentance and to offer the Jews the forgiveness of their sins. The apostles asserted that they and the Holy Spirit were witnesses to all the claims of Jesus.

Luke is the first person in the New Testament to call Jesus "Savior." He uses this word to describe Jesus only once in his Gospel (Luke 2:11), and now he uses it a second time by quoting Peter in his defense of himself and the other apostles before the Sanhedrin.

After Peter's testimony, the assembly went into a paroxysm of rage and was disposed to execute the whole lot of them. But Gamaliel, one of the greatest Hebrew rabbis and a member of the Pharisean party, cautioned them against precipitous action. He said simply that if they were mistaken fanatics, they would in the end destroy themselves, and he cited two recent examples. But if their message was true and what they did was inspired of God, there was really nothing the Sanhedrin could do about it, for God always triumphs. So the body contented itself by beating the apostles with a whip, ordering them again not to speak in the name of Jesus, and then letting them go. The apostles counted themselves fortunate to be able to suffer for Jesus.

The church in Jerusalem had grown so large that the twelve apostles could not handle its business and evangelize and nourish the flock spiritually. Administrative duties distracted them from prayer and the preaching of the word. At the same time the Hellenized Jews of the Dispersion complained that the widows of their deceased brethren were not receiving as much attention as the natives. This complaint no doubt included material support in the form of food and other necessities as well as pastoral care, since the apostles said they did not have time to wait on tables.

To solve this problem, the congregation elected seven men of exemplary character to take on this chore. The remarkable thing is that the congregation chose persons from the group that made the complaint. The seven, as their names indicate, were all Hellenized Jews. These men stood before the apostles who laid their hands on them after prayer and thereby set them apart for this task.

This short passage in Acts is crucial to an understanding of the development of ministry in the church. The apostles were the leaders of the church. Eleven of them had been chosen by Jesus himself at the very beginning of his earthly ministry, and the twelfth had been selected by casting lots between two persons nominated by the congregation. Their qualification was that they had been with Jesus throughout his earthly ministry. They were witnesses to his resurrection. The seven now chosen were to be servants to the apostles, transacting business and performing administrative duties assigned to them. Although they had been elected by the congregation, they could not take office and begin their duties until after the apostles had prayed over them and laid their hands on their heads. The laying on of hands after prayer was the sign of the impartation of the Holy Spirit.

Since the ministry of the seven was that of service, they came to be called *deacons,* which means "servants." Luke describes in this short passage the origin of the diaconate (6:1–6), which was the church's second ministerial order. Up until that point, the apostolate had been the only ministerial order. When the apostles set these seven persons apart for their ministry of service, they performed for the first time the sacred rite of ordination.

That is not to say, however, that because their duties were primarily administrative and functional, they were inferior and had no spiritual quality. The first deacons preached as well. One of them, Stephen, performed miracles and vied with the apostles themselves in the high quality of his ministry. In fact, he exasperated the leaders of several Hellenized synagogues in Jerusalem because he outdid them in debate. Since they could not get the better of him at argumentation, they lied about him, contending that he disparaged both the law and the Temple and thereby blasphemed Moses and God. As a result, he was brought before the Sanhedrin.

In response to the questioning of the high priest, Stephen delivered the longest address recorded in the New Testament other than our Lord's Sermon on the Mount. He turned the tables on his accusers by saying that they had blasphemed Moses by not keeping his law and had defamed the name of God by presuming that God, like some man-made idol, can be confined to a building made of stone.

His speech is a précis of Hebrew history. In one or two places it follows the Samaritan version of the Pentateuch rather than the Hebrew, for example, the age of Terah, Abraham's father, when he died (7:4; see Gen. 11:26, 32; 12:4). Stephen said that Abraham did not leave Haran until after Terah died, but according to the Hebrew version that gives Terah's death at age 205 and Abraham's departure at age 75, Abraham would have left Haran sixty years before Terah died. The Samaritan version, however, states that Terah died at age 145, which is consistent with Stephen's comments. It must have galled the Jewish leaders when Stephen reminded them that Joseph was buried in Shechem among the Samaritans, whom they despised. His review of history was a scathing denunciation of Jewish apostasy, and according to his speech, what the Israelites had been, they were still. He denounced the Sanhedrin for both idolatry and Temple worship.

Stephen must have been a great orator. He spoke passionately, as if he were reliving the events he recounted. Luke says his face was like that of an angel.

When Stephen told his auditors that they were stiff-necked and uncircumcised in heart and ears and that they resisted the Holy Spirit as their fathers had done, it was more than they could take. They gnashed their teeth in rage. Stephen lifted his eyes toward heaven and cried out, "I see the heavens opened, and the Son of man standing on the right hand of God" (7:56). With that, the Jewish leaders rushed him and cast him out of the city and stoned him to death. In the process of throwing the stones, they placed their outer garments at the feet of a young man named Saul. Stephen died, asking God not to lay the sin of murder to the charge of them who slew him. By his death, he became the first martyr of the Christian church.

The martyrdom of Stephen led to a general persecution of the church in Jerusalem. Saul, for example, went from house to house seeking out the Christians and throwing them into prison. Most of the Christians left Jerusalem and sought safety in Judea and Samaria. The apostles, however, stayed in their post of duty with the mother church. This scattering of Christians meant at the same time the dissemination of the gospel. They carried their faith with them and gave it to others wherever they went. The blood of the martyrs became the seed of the church.

CHAPTER FOUR

EVANGELISM IN SAMARIA AND SYRIA

Acts 8:4–12:25

IT SEEMS THAT it took persecution rather than the impetus of the Spirit to shake the Christians loose from their base in Jerusalem and make them carry the gospel to other places and peoples. No doubt God used persecution to accomplish sublime ends. Are we not assured that even the wrath of men shall praise God (Psalm 76:10)? What had happened to Stephen, they assumed, was about to happen to all of them, so they made their way to safety outside the reach of the Sanhedrin. The trauma of Stephen's martyrdom recalled to the apostles our Lord's commission and led to a concerted effort on the part of the leaders in Jerusalem to begin the evangelization of the regions outside Jewish territory. The first places to receive the gospel from the mother church were Samaria and Syria.

Philip the Evangelist (8:4–40)

The first evangelist to proclaim the gospel outside Jerusalem was Philip, who was not one of the apostles. He was only a deacon, one of the seven chosen to relieve the apostles of menial chores. His primary responsibility was to wait on tables. Yet this humble household servant is the first foreign missionary in Christian history. God's ways are mysterious.

Both the first martyr and the first missionary come from the diaconate, not the apostolate.

Philip's first theater of operation as an evangelist was the city of Samaria. It had been the capital of the Northern Kingdom in the heyday of Israel's greatness. It was still the largest city in the territory of the same name. Though Samaria was adjacent to Judea and populated by people of Israelite lineage, the Jews despised the Samaritans and had no dealings with them. Unlike the Jews, the Samaritans had not preserved their racial purity, but had intermingled with the foreigners whom conquerors had sent into the land at the time of the Exile. Their version of the scripture was different from that of the Jews; and their center of worship was Mount Gerizim, not the Temple in Jerusalem. Philip was a Hellenized Jew, but Samaritans proved most receptive to his message, and men and women alike accepted baptism at his hands.

The way had been prepared for Philip by a magician named Simon. He had bewitched the people with sorcery so that they thought of him as "the great power of God" (8:10). Evidently he had by his magic convinced them that he was performing miracles. But Simon's magic conveyed no message, and magic will not heal diseases, expel unclean spirits, overcome palsy, and cure lameness. What Philip did had practical effects on the lives of the people. They benefited physically and mentally from his work. At the same time his miracles carried with them a message, for he talked to the people about the kingdom of God. Even Simon saw the difference, and he, too, accepted baptism. So enthusiastic was he about Philip's ministry that he followed the evangelist about wherever he went. The whole city of Samaria received Philip with joy.

The news of what had happened reached the apostles in Jerusalem, and Peter and John were sent by the mother church to Samaria to confirm the converts in the faith. The Samaritans had received baptism for the remission of their sins, but they had not received the power of the Holy Spirit.

Peter and John supplied this deficiency, for the apostles laid their hands on them, and they received the gift of the Holy Spirit. They had received their first great blessing at the hands of Philip; what they got through the apostles was a second blessing. Outwardly it signified their union with the mother church.

Those who had been ostracized by the Jews were now welcomed by Christ through two of his apostles who were Jews. Philip was a Hellenized Jew; he might even have been a Greek proselyte. But Peter and John were native Jews. Their action in behalf of the Samaritans signalized the passing away of the old Israel with its rites and ceremonies and especially its exclusiveness. The new Israel was coming into being with its inclusiveness; there would be neither Jew nor Samaritan but just brothers and sisters in Christ.

Unfortunately for Simon, the lucrative trade of the magician took precedence over the duties of a disciple of Christ. Though only a convert, he immediately aspired to the honors and privileges of an apostle. He told Peter and John that if they would give him the power to confer the Holy Spirit through the imposition of his hands on whomsoever he chose, he would be more than glad to pay them for it. He knew that by charging people for the gift, he would soon accumulate a fortune.

By making the two apostles that offer, Simon projected his name into the vocabulary of infamy. *Simony* means "the purchase of an eccelesiastical office with money." In J. B. Phillips's literal translation of the Greek text, Peter said to Simon, "To hell with you and your money!" (8:20). The very thought that a gift of God can be purchased with money is repugnant to any sincere Christian. The very request, Peter asserted, shows that Simon, though baptized, was still in the bonds of iniquity. Whether he meant it or not, Simon feigned penitence and asked Peter to pray that he escape the curse of God.

These few facts are all we know about Simon from the

New Testament. However, several of the church fathers provide information about him. According to tradition, he founded a sect of his own as a rival to apostolic Christianity. He ran across Peter again in Rome, where Peter got the better of him in debate. Nonetheless, Simon, claiming to be the earthly personification of God, had his disciples dig a grave and put him in it. He ordered them to cover him with dirt, promising that he would rise again like Jesus Christ. But he never did. Simon was buried alive.

An angel of the Lord directed Philip to take the desert highway to Gaza. It was a most unlikely road on which to encounter prospective converts, but there Philip encountered an Ethiopian eunuch who held the exalted position of treasurer to Queen Candace. The eunuch was in a chariot, presumably drawn by oxen since it was moving so slowly that Philip could walk beside it and converse with its occupant. The man was reading the passage about the Suffering Servant in Isaiah. When he realized Philip was well versed in the scriptures, he invited him to sit beside him in his chariot and interpret the passage. In ancient times people read aloud to themselves. That is how Philip knew the Ethiopian was a devotee of the Hebrew scriptures. He probably was a "God-fearer," one who believed the teachings of the Hebrew religion but could not embrace it as a devotee, and would have been a proselyte had that been possible. The Jewish religion excluded a castrated man from the Temple, so he could not have been formally initiated in the Jewish faith. At most he could receive its blessings only from afar. It would appear that he was interested enough to read its scriptures and even attend its feasts and holy days.

Philip told the eunuch about Jesus, convinced him that Jesus was the fulfillment of the very scripture he was reading, and that no handicap, physical or otherwise, would exclude a person from full fellowship in Christian faith. As soon as they came upon water, the eunuch requested baptism of Philip.

At this period Ethiopia included the Sudan. The eunuch was a black person, so a member of the black race was among the very early recipients of the Christian faith. The inclusion of Africa within the Christian orbit belongs to the very first decade of the Apostolic Age.

Conversion of Saul (9:1–31)

After Luke deposits Philip at Caesarea, which was his home, he shifts attention to Saul, who had witnessed the martyrdom of Stephen and had gone on a personal crusade against the Christians in Jerusalem, invading the privacy of their homes and hauling them away to prison. Now Saul essays to extend his mission of persecution all the way to Damascus, which is 150 miles from Jerusalem and in a different province of the Roman Empire. Indeed, since it belongs to the Decapolis, a league of self-governing cities, it manages its own affairs, though it is in the province of Syria.

Saul secures letters of authorization from the high priest in Jerusalem and intends to bind those Jewish Christians he is able to capture and bring them back to Jerusalem either to languish in prison or perhaps even to suffer the same fate as Stephen. It is hard to understand how he could do this outside the province of Judea unless there was a treaty of extradition between the two communities. Evidently the Syrian Jews were permitted by the government of Damascus to arrest any Jews from Jerusalem who were accused of breaking the law and return them to their native land for trial and punishment. Otherwise, Saul would have had to kidnap them, which would have put him in more jeopardy than they were in. The very fact that he secured letters of authorization indicates that extradition was possible in such cases.

But in this instance, the accuser becomes the accused. Before Saul can reach Damascus, he is struck down by a blinding light and told by a voice from heaven that he is an enemy of God engaged in warfare against God's own people. Saul recognizes the voice as carrying divine authority; there is no uncertainty in his mind about this. And the voice accuses him of persecuting the very One who is speaking to him. When Saul asks for an identification, the speaker identifies himself as Jesus. Saul perceives that the One he has hated and despised as an evil impostor is after all the true Messiah and is now in heaven in the company of God. He realizes with fear and dread that in persecuting the followers of Jesus he is persecuting Jesus and, through him, almighty God.

The story of his conversion is repeated twice in the Acts by Saul, or Paul as he is by then called, first, in defense of himself before the mob in Jerusalem (22:3–16) and, second, in his testimony before Festus and King Agrippa in Caesarea (26:4–18). All three accounts vary as to details. Paul includes certain things in what he says to Festus and Agrippa that he leaves out when he speaks to the mob. But there are no contradictions in either of the subsequent accounts. However, there seems to be a contradiction at one point between them and the first account. They say that those with Saul saw the light but heard no voice (22:9; 26:14); the first account states that the men journeying with Saul did indeed hear a voice (9:7), but it does not say whether they saw the light or not. At least, if they did, the light did not blind them, for they led Saul into the city. This seeming discrepancy is minor, and perhaps is no discrepancy at all. Paul in his personal account probably meant that they did not hear what the heavenly voice was saying to him, and Luke in the first account may mean by the word *voice* that these companions heard no more than a loud noise.

There was already a Christian community in Damascus when Saul got there. In it no doubt were the converts from Jerusalem he had come to apprehend. That is why Ananias, their leader, was hesitant to go to Saul to help him. But God told him to go, and away he went. He called Saul "brother," he said that the same Jesus whom Saul encountered on the road to Damascus had sent him, and he put his hands on Saul's head. Immediately Saul was relieved of his blindness. He accepted baptism at the hands of Ananias and was made a part of the Christian community.

Though Luke does not tell us this in the Acts, Paul says that he went into Arabia, no doubt to be alone with God and meditate on his experience and seek guidance (Gal. 1:17). He returned to Damascus and by his testimony upset the Jews in the city. They planned to kill him, but his friends enabled him to escape at night by letting him down in a basket from the top of the city's wall. Then, he went to Jerusalem for the first time since his conversion.

That was three years after his conversion (Gal. 1:18). Even so, the followers of Jesus in Jerusalem still feared him, remembering how he had persecuted them. They doubted his sincerity, thought his claim to be a Christian was only a pretense, and believed he was really a spy planted by the Jewish authorities in their community.

Only Barnabas was convinced of his sincerity. After Barnabas had marshaled all the facts, he told the Christian leaders about what Saul had gone through since he left Jerusalem and about his boldness in witnessing to Christ in Damascus. At least two of them received him, for Paul himself tells us that he spent fifteen days with Peter and talked with James, the Lord's brother (Gal. 1:18–19). He did, however, preach Christ publicly in Jerusalem and debate with Grecian proselytes, who were so offended by him that they plotted to kill him. To protect him, the Christian community arranged for his passage by ship from Caesarea to Tarsus, which was his home. Only after he left was peace restored to the Christians in Jerusalem and the neighboring regions of Judea, Galilee, and Samaria. The Holy Spirit comforted them. They were free to evangelize, and the church continued to grow.

Paul thought of his experience on the road to Damascus

as a personal encounter with Jesus, comparable to Jesus' postresurrection experiences with the disciples. He claims that he met Jesus there and that Jesus made him an apostle. The risen Christ commissioned him to the apostolate just as he had commissioned the twelve disciples during his earthly ministry, and Paul felt that his commission was just as valid as theirs (1 Cor. 15:8–11).

Peter Among the Gentiles (9:32–11:18)

Before Saul made his momentous trip to Jerusalem after his conversion and spent most of his time there with Peter, who was chief among the apostles, the Holy Spirit had prepared Peter to receive him and give him good counsel in the propagation of the gospel. Though Paul is known as the apostle to the gentiles, Peter is the one who initiated the mission to the gentiles. To be sure, the deacon Philip had converted and baptized the first gentile in the person of the Ethiopian eunuch. But that seems to have been an isolated incident in the life of the church. Philip did not follow it up, nor did the apostles send any evangelists into Ethiopia to build on the eunuch's experience.

When Peter, however, proclaimed the gospel to the Roman centurion Cornelius, he incorporated him and as many others as believed into the church and thereby changed the policy of the church. It was no longer a collection of Jews and proselytes who accepted Jewish rites and customs but was open to all races and peoples on equal terms, so long as they accepted Jesus Christ as their Savior.

Peter had been on an apostolic visit to the followers of Jesus outside Jerusalem. At Lydda, he had cured Aeneas, who had been afflicted with palsy for eight years, and at Joppa, he had raised Dorcas, or Tabitha, from the dead. He stayed many days at Joppa, where he was the guest of Simon, a tanner by trade.

Nearby at Caesarea on the seacoast, which was the Roman capital of Judea when it was ruled by a procurator such as Pontius Pilate had been, there were stationed Roman troops. Cornelius was a centurion, a high-ranking noncommissioned officer similar to a sergeant or perhaps a low-ranking commissioned officer like a second lieutenant in the U.S. Army. Cornelius had been in that part of the empire long enough to become familiar with the Jewish religion, and he was deeply impressed by it and its high standard of morality. He was not, however, a proselyte. He was a "God-fearer," a person who accepted monotheism and aspired to lead a worthy life, and he was known for giving generously to the poor. One afternoon, about three o'clock, he had a vision of an angel, who told him to send to Joppa for a man named Peter and who gave him directions on how to find Peter. The next day he sent two servants and a faithful soldier to Joppa to get Peter.

On the day of their arrival, Peter was praying at noon on the rooftop of the house where he was staying. Suddenly, he became very hungry and fell sound asleep. He had a dream in which a big sheet full of all kinds of animals was let down before him, and a voice out of heaven instructed him to kill and eat. Peter was horrified. Never in his whole life had he violated the dietary prescriptions of Moses. Anything other than kosher was unclean to him. But the voice, which he took to be the voice of God, said that nothing God has made is common and unclean.

After Peter awoke, the arrival of the men from Caesarea was announced. When he learned their mission, he discerned immediately the meaning of his dream. They stayed overnight, and the next day he and some others went with them to the house of Cornelius in Caesarea. Cornelius, anticipating Peter's coming, had collected the members of his family and other friends and acquaintances to meet him. Cornelius ran out ahead to greet Peter and fell at his feet. Peter lifted him up, saying, "Don't do this. I am just a man as you are." He went on to say, "You know that it is not lawful for a Jew to visit in the home of a gentile, but God told me not to look on any person as common and unclean" (10:26–28, AP).

Peter preached to the assembled group. As a result of his sermon, the entire group had an experience of the Holy Spirit similar to that of the disciples on the day of Pentecost. Peter's companions who were Jews were amazed that the Holy Spirit would descend on gentiles. Peter then directed his Jewish companions to baptize them, and he and they stayed in Cornelius's house.

It is important to note that baptism does not produce regeneration. It is the other way around. The Holy Spirit comes first and brings conversion. Baptism is only the outward sign that the experience has taken place.

The news of what Peter had done was not received very well by the brethren in Jerusalem or in the outlying regions throughout Judea. Their attitude was the same as what Peter's had been prior to his vision. They were all circumcised Jews who, like Peter, had kept Moses' dietary laws all their lives. They were aghast that he, a Jew, would condescend to eat and sleep under the same roof with gentiles. Thus, as soon as he returned to Jerusalem, they took issue with him. Those who in the King James Version of Acts are called "they that were of the circumcision" (11:2) are thereby clearly described. This translation is more accurate than that in the Revised Standard Version, which reads "circumcision party," as if there had been such a party in the early church in opposition to an "uncircumcision party." All the phrase means is Jewish Christians, and these constituted all of them. If parties later arose over this issue, this was the occasion that produced them. There was no thought about this prior to Peter's action.

Peter's response to their criticism was simply to recount in a straightforward manner what had happened, beginning with his vision and going on to Cornelius's vision and the natural correspondence in meaning between them. The result that took place when he and Cornelius acted in compliance with their visions was indisputable proof of the divine authority behind both.

The gentiles received the same gift of the Holy Spirit that the Jewish disciples had received at Pentecost. Thus, gentiles are not second-class citizens in God's kingdom; they have the same first-class citizenship as the Jews. "As I began to speak," said Peter, "the Holy Ghost fell on them, as on us at the beginning" (11:15). Jewish rites and ceremonies and Hebrew blood, race, and ancestry have nothing whatever to do with becoming and being a Christian. All that is required is that one believe on the Lord Jesus Christ by faith and receive the gift of the Holy Spirit. Peter stated, "Forasmuch then as God gave them the like gift as he did unto us, who believed on the Lord Jesus Christ; what was I, that I could withstand God?" (11:17).

The Jewish Christians in Jerusalem had no reply. Peter's argument was irrefutable. But there is no evidence they did anything about it either. The missionary base of Christianity shifts from Jerusalem to Antioch.

Antioch (11:19–30)

Antioch was the third largest city in the Roman Empire, surpassed in population only by Alexandria in Egypt and by Rome itself, the capital and metropolis of the empire. Antioch was the capital of the Roman province of Syria, a thriving commercial center, in fact, the greatest city in Asia Minor. (The Far East and its civilizations were unknown to the Romans.) It was ideally situated to become the center of expanding Christianity.

Christianity first reached Antioch as a result of the persecution in Jerusalem following the stoning of Stephen. Some of the Jews of the Dispersion who had been converted while in Jerusalem but who resided in Antioch returned home. Others, permanent residents in Jerusalem, fled with them and settled in Antioch. They carried their newfound faith with them and began immediately to convert other Jews residing in the city. Soon there was quite a sizable collection of Jewish Christians in Antioch.

In course of time these Jewish Christians began to win persons who were not Jewish to Christ. Unfortunately, Luke does not tell us how this came about. Two factors must have precipitated this evangelistic action on their part. First, Jews of the Dispersion were a minority in the cities where they resided outside the homeland. In order to make a living they had to deal with the majority of other races and religions. They were therefore much more tolerant and adaptable than the Jews at home. Necessity forced them to give to and take from their gentile neighbors. Since Jesus meant everything to them, they were convinced that he might mean something to their gentile friends as well. Second, they heard of Peter's mission to Cornelius and through it the conversion of gentiles in Caesarea. If Peter had been permitted by God to go to the gentiles, surely it was all right for them to do the same. Therefore, in absentia Peter initiated the gentile mission in Antioch so that the infant church in Antioch was composed of both Jews and gentiles.

News of the evangelistic successes eventually reached Jerusalem. The Jerusalem church sent Barnabas, a Cypriot Jew in the city at the time and a Christian leader, as its emissary to Antioch, indicating its intention as the mother church to supervise the activities of all its children. God evidently had other intentions, for Barnabas, rather than instructing and guiding the Antiochians, joined with them and facilitated their work among the gentiles. He even went to Tarsus and solicited the aid of Saul, whom he had met when Saul came from Damascus to Jerusalem and whom he had introduced to Peter and James, the brother of Jesus. Apparently he had been greatly impressed by Saul and felt he would add much to the evangelistic mission in Antioch.

Both Barnabas and Saul won the confidence of the Christians in Antioch. When a famine was predicted, Barnabas and Saul were sent by the church in Antioch to the mother church in Jerusalem with a handsome relief offering for Christians in need in Judea. This is the reverse of what we are familiar with today, when the founding churches send money to support the missionary churches they have established. In the first century the missionary churches had to help their parent in Jerusalem. The wealthy Christians resided in Antioch.

Luke pays Barnabas the highest compliment he pays anybody about whom he writes in the book of Acts when he applies the adjective *good* to him. The Christians first got that name in Antioch; the populace called them that after the name of their Savior. Barnabas helped them most to acquire that name, for he himself was most like Christ.

Herod Agrippa I and Peter (12:1–25)

When Barnabas and Saul arrived in Jerusalem with the collection the church in Antioch had raised for the mother church, they found the Christians in the Holy City in a state of disarray bordering on panic. One of the apostles had been executed, and another, Peter, the prince of the apostles and the recognized leader of the entire Christian movement, was in prison. The conditions that existed at the time of the stoning of Stephen were being repeated but in a more effective and virulent form. Previously, the religious authorities had persecuted the Christians; now it was the secular government, which had the means to do a more thorough and extensive job of it. The probability was that the entire Christian movement in Judea would be annihilated.

The first persecution had struck only at the diaconate. Stephen, the first Christian martyr, was a deacon. But the second martyr, the victim of persecution by the government, was the Apostle James, the son of Zebedee and the brother of John, one of the three on whom Jesus had most depended during his earthly ministry. In fact, Jesus had taken James to the Mount of Transfiguration, and he had asked James to watch and pray while he prayed during those agonizing hours in the Garden of Gethsemane. According to tradition, poor James died within a decade after the resurrection. His brother, John, lived half a century more in order to write his Gospel and preside as bishop over the church in Ephesus. Peter, who shared with James and John this place of preeminence in our Lord's earthly ministry, was targeted for the same fate as James and was languishing in prison awaiting execution.

The person responsible for this disaster was Herod Agrippa I. He was the grandson of Herod the Great, and he, more than anyone else in the Herodian family, had inherited the first Herod's cunning and inordinate gift for amassing power. When Herod the Great died, his kingdom was divided among his three sons, one of whom had been deposed and his tetrarchy put under direct Roman rule through a procurator sent out from the capital.

Herod Agrippa, however, had spent his youth in Rome. There he had become a friend and companion to members of the imperial family, especially Caligula, in whose debaucheries he shared. As a result, Caligula favored him. And even the virtuous Claudius continued that favor; like his grandfather, Agrippa knew how to switch loyalties quickly and make his new superior believe that he had been his admirer and supporter all along. Gradually he acquired the two tetrarchies of Herod Antipas and Philip and even the Roman procuratorship of Judea itself, so at this time he was ruler of all the territory of his grandfather Herod the Great.

In order to curry favor with the Jews and show his devotion to the Temple, Agrippa staged his own persecution of the Judean Christians. He struck at the church's highest leadership, believing that if the heads of the church fell, the whole organization would fall with them. Thus, he executed James and planned to execute Peter as well.

But the Lord had other plans. While the little Christian community prayed fervently for Peter, God sent an angel into the prison at night. The angel miraculously released Peter and deposited him safely in the streets of Jerusalem, where he made his way to the home of Mary, the mother of John Mark and sister of Barnabas. The Christians had assembled there to pray. When the servant came running in to say that Peter was standing outside at the door, they thought that the execution had taken place and that it was Peter's ghost the servant had seen.

Peter entered the house and reassured them. Their prayers had been answered, even though they had obviously not believed that would occur. If they had believed, they would have realized that it was Peter knocking at the door. After an evening of testimony and fellowship with them, Peter made his escape from Jerusalem. The unfortunate guards at the prison paid for Peter's escape with their lives.

Herod Agrippa paid with his life for his persecution of the Christians. There was a Roman festival in Caesarea, probably commemorating Claudius's return from the conquest of Britain. These festivals were no doubt held in all the provinces of the empire. On the second day of the festival Agrippa appeared in the theater erected by his grandfather. It was crowded beyond capacity. The king's robe was made of silver threads, and its shining in the sunlight dazzled the crowd. The king seemed too magnificent to be human, and people acknowledged him to be a god. The king was overcome by the flattery of his people, though he knew what the law said: "Thou shalt have no other gods before me" (Exod. 20:3). Almost immediately the king fell before the multitude. He was carried to his palace, and within a week he was dead, his body infested with worms as had been that of his grandfather, Herod the Great. Based on these symptoms, he probably died of tertiary syphilis contracted during his licentious youth with Caligula in Rome.

Herod Agrippa I died in A.D. 44. But Peter had already left Jerusalem. God used Herod's tyranny to release Peter for wider service throughout the empire. Nonetheless, Herod paid for his tyranny and corruption with his life.

Secular history helps us establish dates of importance in sacred history. All the events recorded in the first twelve chapters of the Acts of the Apostles took place within a span of only fourteen years, from Pentecost in A.D. 30 to the death of Herod Agrippa and Peter's exodus from Jerusalem in A.D. 44. We know Saul spent one year working with Barnabas in Antioch before going to Jerusalem with the offering for the Christians there (11:26). Three years elapsed between his conversion and his return to Jerusalem from Damascus after he had become a Christian (Gal. 1:18). What we do not know is how long Saul stayed in Tarsus, where he went after this first visit to Jerusalem, when he talked off and on for fifteen days with Peter, and the time Barnabas brought him to Antioch. This could have been anywhere from one to three years. If it was only one year, then Saul was converted in A.D. 39; if three years, then in A.D. 37. The amazing fact is that Saul was converted less than a decade after the death and resurrection of Jesus and the descent of the Holy Spirit on the disciples at Pentecost.

CHAPTER FIVE

THE ANTIOCHENE MISSION

Acts 13:1–16:7

CHRISTENDOM IS INDEBTED to the church at Antioch for conceiving of world missions as an obligation of the gospel and for devising the grand missionary strategy that gradually would embrace the world. To be sure, the church is beholden to Peter for first witnessing for Christ to a Roman household and therefore breaking the barrier between Jew and gentile. But it was in Antioch, where Christianity got its name, that the initiative was taken by a local congregation to support a missionary enterprise to peoples beyond its own locale. Heretofore the gospel had spread almost accidentally—that is, as a result of Christians moving to different parts of the country to escape persecution or migrating for business purposes, always carrying their faith with them. But due to the Antiochene resolve, the propagation of the gospel becomes a deliberate policy of the church.

Consequently, the book of Acts exemplifies a different literary purpose after chapter 12. It tells the story of the faith from a new perspective with the beginning of chapter 13. The author's interest is now primarily with the conversion of the gentiles. Luke focuses the light of history on Paul, not on Peter. Though his book is still the Gospel of the Holy Spirit, the Spirit works through the missionary activity of Paul and his associates.

The First Missionary Journey (13:1–14:28)

The church in Antioch was charismatic. It sought the direct guidance of the Holy Spirit, and that guidance came as a result of fasting and prayer and from the lips of designated teachers and prophets, five of whom Luke names. Barnabas is the first one listed to indicate his preeminence, and Saul is the last. Simeon and Lucius were both from Cyrene. Simeon bears also the name Niger, which probably indicates that he was black. We know nothing more of Lucius. Manaen had been prominent in the secular world as a companion of Herod the tetrarch; most commentators assume this to have been Herod Antipas. If so, Manaen was a young man in Herod's court during the ministry of Jesus and probably witnessed the beheading of John the Baptist.

As a result of the advice of these five individuals, the Antiochene church chose Barnabas and Saul to be its first missionaries. Just as we still do today, the people of the church laid hands on them and thereby consecrated them as missionaries. This was an act of churchly blessing. Since Barnabas was in charge of the mission, they went first to Cyprus, for he was a Cypriot. Barnabas's nephew, young John Mark, accompanied them.

Their stay in Cyprus seems to have been of short duration. They landed at Salamis, preached to the Jews in the synagogues there, presumably with no noticeable results, and traveled to Paphos, the Roman capital of the island. There their mission began to succeed, for they won the attention and respect of the Roman ruler of the island, Sergius Paulus, whose heart was hungry for the word of God.

Their means of access to him was strange and even frightening. They had been obstructed in their mission by a sorcerer named Bar-Jesus nicknamed Elymas, which means "magician." Saul looked Elymas straight in the eyes and either hypnotized him so that he thought he was blind or else blinded him outright, for he could not see how to walk and had to be led away. The blindness was only temporary and wore away after Barnabas and Saul accomplished their purpose.

At this point in his narrative, Luke ceases to call Barnabas's companion by his Jewish name "Saul" and starts calling him by his Roman name "Paul," thus anticipating his mission to the gentiles (13:9). From that point, Paul appears to have been the chief spokesman for the mission. Presumably he takes over the leadership of the enterprise from Barnabas. If so, it must have been by Barnabas's consent in that he recognized Paul to be better at evangelism than he. The two missionaries won Sergius Paulus to the faith, for Luke tells us he believed the doctrine of the Lord.

Cyprus is 140 miles long and 60 miles wide, about the size of ancient Israel. Evidently the missionaries felt they had finished there, for from Paphos they sailed to the coast of what is today Turkey and what was then Pamphylia. The port at which they landed was Perga. Apparently John Mark, Barnabas's nephew, had not wanted to leave Cyprus so soon, or else had not wanted to make the journey at all; he deserted the mission at Perga and returned to Jerusalem.

Perga in Pamphylia was only the gateway for Paul and Barnabas to the interior. They proceeded immediately to Pisidian Antioch where they attended the synagogue on the sabbath day, as was their custom. After the reading of the law and the prophets, the ruler of the synagogue asked them if they had anything to say. This request was not unusual in that day. The synagogue was not like the Temple, with its sacrifices and ceremonial rites. Worship in the synagogue was far less formal. Anyone who was capable of doing so could be invited by the person in charge of the service to expatiate on the scripture readings for the day.

Paul, who had studied under Gamaliel in Jerusalem, was eminently qualified to do so. We do not know what the lessons for that sabbath were, but we do know what Paul said, for Luke gives us a full account of his message. Paul focuses on the rule of David and David's special place in God's affections. He then makes the claim that Jesus, a direct descendant of David, is the fulfillment of God's promise to Israel to send a Savior.

Immediately Paul and Barnabas collected from the congregation a group of followers. The officials of the synagogue were at first undecided in their reaction to Paul, but they permitted him to speak again on the next sabbath. However, when practically the entire city turned out to hear him and he was able to make converts while they were not, they became intensely jealous of him and began to stir up so much opposition to him and Barnabas that they were expelled from Pisidian Antioch.

They fared little better in Iconium. That city divided almost evenly over them, half supporting them and the other half bitterly opposing them. But when overtures were made to the rulers of the city for permission to stone them, Paul and Barnabas fled to Lystra and Derbe.

At Lystra, Paul not only preached effectively, but he performed a miracle, which had astonishing results. As Paul preached, there was a man listening who had been lame in his feet since birth and was unable to walk. Paul noticed the intensity with which the man listened, so he turned to him and commanded him to walk. The cure of the lame man produced a sensation among the gentiles of the city.

Devotees of Roman deities that the Romans had borrowed from the Greeks, the gentiles thought Paul and Barnabas were gods masquerading as men. Barnabas was the silent partner of the two, but was tall and stately in appearance; Paul did all the talking, but was smaller and less prepossessing than his companion. Thus, they took Barnabas to be Jupiter, the supreme god, and Paul to be Mercury, the messenger and spokesman of the gods. There was a temple to Jupiter in Lystra, and its priest fell in with the populace, bringing with them garlands and oxen to make sacrifice to Barnabas and his companion Paul, believing as they did that they were Jupiter and Mercury. As we know from mythology, it was the habit of Jupiter to wander the earth in the form of man, animal, or bird and thereby make contact with human beings. Paul and Barnabas disclaimed for themselves any form of divinity, protesting that they were just as human as their would-be worshipers.

The people's disappointment over this admission and their mistake made them vulnerable to the accusations against Paul and Barnabas from Jews who came from Iconium and Antioch, so they stoned Paul and left him for dead. Nonetheless, when Paul recovered, he and Barnabas had the courage not only to proceed to Derbe to preach the gospel there, but to retrace their steps to Lystra, Iconium, and Pisidian Antioch, confirming the converts they had made in those cities in the faith and establishing local congregations therein. They appointed elders—that is, local pastors to care for each congregation. When the Jews rejected Paul and Barnabas at Pisidian Antioch, Paul turned away from the recalcitrant Jews to preach the gospel to the more receptive gentiles.

The two returned via Perga, where they preached the gospel, and Attalia to Antioch to report on their first missionary journey.

The Gentile Problem and Its Solution (15:1–35)

Next to the description of Pentecost in the second chapter of Acts, this passage is the most important in the entire book, for what takes place here opens up for the church its largest field for expansion and makes possible the eventual winning of the Roman Empire to Christianity. It delineates an historical watershed: the transformation of Christianity from a small Jewish sect into an independent and autonomous church.

After the return of Paul and Barnabas from their missionary journey together, certain men from Jerusalem arrived in Antioch and insisted that circumcision is essential to Christian salvation, thus making the grace of God through Jesus Christ subsidiary to the Mosaic law and making the Savior himself dependent on Moses. To settle the matter, the church at Antioch sent a delegation, headed by Paul and Barnabas, to the mother church in Jerusalem to ascertain from the apostles and elders the position of the church in the matter.

Though this is a disputed issue in New Testament historiography, it is my opinion that this trip was Paul's third visit to Jerusalem after his conversion and subsequent to the arresting argumentation and debate Paul recounts in Galatians 2:1–10. For one thing, the meeting described in Galatians was a private one between Paul and Peter, John, and the Lord's brother, James (Gal. 2:2, 9), while this one was a public meeting between Paul and the Jerusalem congregation. After the issue was decided by this public Jerusalem Conference, it would have been well nigh impossible for James to take the restrictive Jewish attitude he did toward the Christian gentiles in Antioch (Gal. 2:12) and for his emissaries to frighten Peter to the extent that he withdrew from the table with gentiles and caused even Barnabas to do the same (Gal. 2:11–15).

These events described in Galatians had to occur before the adjudication of this dispute by the Jerusalem Conference, and in all probability did occur before Paul and Barnabas made their missionary journey. If this was the case, it would have allowed ample time for James to change his mind and Peter to support publicly what he had already done privately, so that both of them were able to take the progressive stands they did at the Jerusalem Conference.

The real problem lies at the point of the fourteen years that Paul says elapsed between the visit he made to Jerusalem after his conversion and the time he argued privately with Peter, John, and James. His second visit to Jerusalem, with the collection taken in Antioch for the brethren in Jerusalem in anticipation of the famine (Acts 11:27–30), which I believe was the time of his private disputation as described in Galatians 2:1–10, is a rather long span of time to allow between his first and second visits. In fact, it is too long to correspond with the date of Herod Agrippa's death, by means of which we are able on the basis of Luke's information to date his second visit. Chronologically considered, the events described in Galatians 2:1–10 fit perfectly with this third visit, and traditionally Luke's account of the Jerusalem Conference and Paul's account of his meeting with the two apostles and James, the Lord's brother, in Galatians describe the same event.

Be that as it may, Paul (according to Luke) plays little part in the decision of the Jerusalem Conference. All he and Barnabas do is describe what happened in regard to the gentiles on their missionary journey. Peter is the first to respond and contend, on the basis of his experience in the conversion of Cornelius, that God makes no difference between Jews and gentiles but gives the Holy Spirit equally to both when they accept God's grace through the Lord Jesus Christ.

James lends his masterful support as a conservative Jewish Christian to the same position by fortifying it with reference to the prophet Amos, who says that the Lord will build again the tabernacle of David, which is fallen down, and will gather therein all the gentiles (James in Acts substitutes "Gentiles" for Amos's "heathen") who are called by God's name (Amos 9:11–12). The fact that James quotes Amos from the Greek Septuagint version of the Hebrew scripture rather than the Hebrew would indicate that Luke in recalling James's speech used the Greek text with which he was familiar. It is not likely that James could have read Greek or ever have seen the Septuagint version, which was translated from Hebrew into Greek in Alexandria, Egypt.

The decision reached was that gentiles are equal in all religious matters to Jews, for both are alike dependent on the grace of God in Jesus Christ for salvation. The Mosaic law alone is no more sufficient for Jewish Christians than it is for gentile Christians. The only caveat to the decision was that gentiles restrain from eating things strangled or meat with blood left in it. This was no doubt to accommodate Jews who adhered strictly to the Mosaic dietary prescriptions so that they might conveniently eat with gentile Christians. Evidently, Paul was willing to accede to this, as he did not want to do anything that would needlessly cause offense (Rom. 14:19–21; 1 Cor. 10:23–33). Naturally, the moral law had to be upheld by gentiles just as much as by Jews, so that the prohibitions against idolatry and fornication belong to the teachings of Jesus as well as the law of Moses.

A formal letter was drawn up to announce the decision of the Jerusalem church and was sent back to Antioch by two emissaries, Judas Barsabbas and Silas, both prophets, along with Paul and Barnabas, beloved by the church because they had risked their lives for Jesus Christ. The church had been apprised of Paul's stoning at Lystra and of his and Barnabas's going back over hostile territory on that first missionary journey, thereby endangering their lives. The formal letter contained the restriction of eating any food offered to idols— that is, meat put on the market by pagan priests after they had used it in their sacrifices. This could have been a further concession to the tender feelings of Jewish Christians, but it might well have been just as much a precaution to gentile Christians against making any contacts with pagan worship in any form.

After Judas and Silas had fulfilled their mission in Antioch, the Antiochene church gave them permission to leave, but Silas chose to remain.

The Separation of Paul and Barnabas (15:36–16:7)

Paul proposed to Barnabas, after they had spent some time in Antioch, that they return to all the cities they had evangelized during their first missionary journey. Barnabas readily consented. But when they began to make arrangements for the trip, they had a disagreement about whether John Mark should accompany them. Barnabas insisted that they take him. Paul refused. Barnabas, being a generous and kindly disposed person, wanted to give young Mark a second chance. Paul, concerned only for the success of the enterprise, did not want to risk a second defection from Mark. Mark was kin to Barnabas; and though Barnabas was fond of Paul, the two men separated over this issue.

Barnabas and Mark sailed to Cyprus. Paul chose Silas to accompany him, and they departed north through Syria and Cilicia, which Paul had evangelized when he had returned to Tarsus from Damascus before Barnabas went to fetch him for work in Antioch. From Cilicia, they passed through a sharp and treacherous defile in the mountains known as the Cilician Gates into southern Galatia. This route, in contrast to the route from Perga through Pisidian Antioch, brought them first to Derbe and from there to Lystra.

There lived in Lystra with his mother and grandmother, both Jewish Christians, a young convert to Christianity named Timothy, whose father was a gentile. Presumably Paul had converted all three of them on his first missionary journey. Now he wanted Timothy as his traveling companion. In mixed marriages between Jews and gentiles, the Jews expected the offspring to be reared as Jews and to keep all the prescriptions of the Hebrew law. Timothy, probably because of objections from his father, had never been circumcised. Therefore, he was considered illegitimate by the Jews. They disdained him as a bastard, though he was an honorable man and highly respected in Lystra and even Iconium. To satisfy

Jewish prejudice, Paul circumcised him, even though at the time he publicized the edict of the church in Jerusalem regarding gentiles.

Paul took Timothy with him and Silas, and after visiting all the churches in the region, they went down into Mysia to the coast and would have gone north into Bithynia, but the Holy Spirit prevented them.

CHAPTER SIX

THE MISSION TO GREECE

Acts 16:8–18:22

THE SECOND MISSIONARY JOURNEY began, as we have seen, with Paul's revisiting the churches he had established on his first missionary journey. He omitted Cyprus and took a different itinerary into lower Galatia, which is now the upper region of southwestern Turkey. His approach to the cities he had visited before was different, but the places themselves were the same.

Now, however, this second missionary journey takes a different turn altogether. Paul abandons the Asiatic continent and moves westward into Europe. There is no indication in Acts that he sought the guidance of the Holy Spirit when he began this second missionary journey. He just seems to have assumed that it was God's will for him to check up on the churches he had established and to assure himself of their moral and spiritual well-being. His sponsoring congregation in Antioch had evidently assumed the same thing, for it had sent him out again with its blessings.

At this juncture, the Holy Spirit takes the initiative and intervenes. If Paul won't consult the Holy Spirit, then the Holy Spirit will advise Paul and tell him exactly what to do. From this point, Paul seems not to be under the direction of the church of Antioch but to be led entirely by the Holy Spirit. From an earthly perspective, he seems to be an independent missionary.

Macedonia (16:8–17:15)

At Troas, which was close to the Troy of Homer's *Iliad,* that fabled city to which Paris had allured Helen and against which the Greeks fought under her wronged husband, Menelaus, in order to bring her home again, Paul had a dream of a Macedonian beseeching him to cross the sea to Macedonia and help him and his people. In antiquity, revelation often came to prophets and seers through dreams. Certainly Paul took the Macedonian's entreaty as a divine command.

As Paul accepts the invitation and prepares to go, Luke introduces for the first time in the text of Acts what has come to be known as the "we passages" (16:10). The traditional interpretation of these passages is that Luke, the narrator, is present as a member of Paul's company and an actual participant in what he is writing about. I find no evidence to contradict this assumption. At Troas, it would seem that Luke the gentile has been added to Silas and Timothy as one of Paul's traveling companions.

The little group sails via the island of Samothrace and lands at Neapolis, the port for Philippi, which is only 10 miles away. They had covered a distance of only 125 miles, though Macedonia is separated from Mysia by the Ionian Sea. Philippi, named for Philip, the father of Alexander the Great, had under the Romans become a colony for retired soldiers who had to pay no imperial taxes and received many benefits in appreciation for their military services to the empire. Consequently, very few Jews were there, and those that were there were despised by the citizenry. It took ten men, according to Jewish law, to organize a synagogue. Presumably there were not enough men for Philippi to have a synagogue, for the Jews met outside town by a riverbank for their prayers. When Paul and his group discovered them on the sabbath day, only women were present.

A godly person among them was Lydia from Thyatira in Asia Minor. She sold exquisite purple cloth that she imported from her native city, which was famous in the Hellenistic world for its purple dye and the cloth it exported in that color. Lydia responded to Paul's message and accepted baptism from him. Indeed, he converted her whole household, and she invited him and his party to be guests in her home.

Lydia has the honor of being the first person converted by Paul to Christianity on European soil. It was in her home, no doubt, that the first Christian congregation in Europe was to meet and the first church in Europe was to be organized. Philippi has the distinction of being the Holy Spirit's beachhead on the continent of Europe, the place where Paul began his European ministry.

Paul's recognition by the general public in Philippi came about under most unusual circumstances. As he and his company went to prayer, they were accosted by a young woman, presumably a slave, for Luke tells us she brought her masters money through her gifts as a fortune teller. She told Paul's fortune gratuitously—that is, without his soliciting her services. As he would pass her on the street, she would cry out so that all could hear: "This man and his companions are servants of the most high God, and they can show us the way to salvation" (16:17, AP). This performance went on over a period of several days, and Paul got tired of it. He realized that her gift was in reality a curse, for she was possessed with a spirit of divination. The spirit threw her into an unnatural state, which enabled her to make these predictions. So one day after she cried out after Paul, the apostle turned to her and exorcised her of the spirit of divination.

With the spirit gone, she lost her gift of fortune telling and thereby became profitless to her masters. They were incensed over their financial loss. What had been a profit for them became a liability. They therefore arraigned Paul and Silas before the city magistrates, complaining that they had fomented a disturbance in the city. In reality the only persons Paul and Silas had disturbed were the few men who owned the girl and had been deprived of their revenue by the exorcism Paul had exerted on her. But they were careful to conceal this under their general complaint that these two had caused trouble to the citizenry in general. They were accused of introducing customs that were unlawful for Romans to observe. The owners of the slave girl incited a mob.

When this happened, the magistrates became agitated. They had Paul and Silas beaten and then thrown into prison with stipulation to the jailer that they be kept safely. The jailer understood this to mean that their crime was such as to require maximum security. He must have thought that they were dangerous revolutionaries because he put them in the stocks within the inner prison. Luke and Timothy were not involved, so the "we passages" of Acts stop temporarily with the Philippian imprisonment.

At midnight, while Paul and Silas were recovering from the horrible beating that had been inflicted on them, the jail rocked under the impact of an earthquake, and all the doors of the prison were thrown ajar. When the warden of the prison realized what had happened and supposed that the prisoners had taken advantage of the earthquake and had escaped, he started to commit suicide. To be sure, Roman law held that a jailer was responsible for the safekeeping of his prisoners. If any escaped due to his negligence, he had to compensate to the state for their escape with his life. But the jailer could hardly be held responsible for an earthquake; and Rome, being famous for her justice, would hardly have punished the jailer for the results of something over which he had no control. Nonetheless, Luke says he was about to commit suicide when Paul called to him and assured him that the prisoners were all there and every one of them could be accounted for.

With this information, the warden no doubt recalled the announcement of the little fortune teller before her gift of divination had been taken from her: "These men are the servants of the most high God" (16:17), for he commanded a light and went to Paul and Silas and asked them what he must do to be saved. Paul gave him the answer: "Believe on the Lord Jesus Christ, and thou shalt be saved" (16:31). This, as all Paul's utterances and writings testify, is the only means of salvation. Luke says that Paul and Silas spoke to him and his household the word of the Lord. As a result, he and his household were converted and baptized, and Paul and Silas were made guests for the rest of the night in the jailer's home.

Lydia and her household had been Paul's first European converts. Before conversion, they had been Jewish proselytes. Now a Roman official and his household had been won by Paul to the Christian faith.

The magistrates sent word the next morning to release the prisoners. But they had overstepped their authority in punishing Roman citizens. Therefore, Paul would not be released until they came in person to him. After the public act of apology, he and Silas returned to Lydia's house, met with the infant church, and left the town.

Rome had covered her empire with a network of fine roads, linking major cities and terminating at ports from which vessels sailed directly to Italy. One of these roads was the Via Egnatia, which ran from Byzantium through the port of Neapolis on the east coast of Macedonia to Dyrrhachium on the west coast and served the cities and towns in between. Paul and his companions took this highway through Amphipolis and Apollonia and came directly to Thessalonica, which was the capital and chief city of the province of Macedonia.

Paul stayed there for at least three weeks, for Luke tells us that he spent three successive sabbaths at the Thessalonian synagogue reasoning with the congregation out of the Hebrew scripture that their Messiah had to suffer and die and rise from the dead and that Jesus had done all these things and was therefore that Messiah. Paul had to provide for his needs by working; he refused to accept handouts from those to whom he preached (1 Thess. 2:9) except the hospitality that a man named Jason extended to him by keeping him in his home. Jason, as his name would imply, was probably a gentile, perhaps even a Roman. His house was likely the place where the first Christian congregation in Thessalonica was organized, and his family its nucleus.

The Jews, who could not get the better of Paul through argument, stirred up a mob of lewd persons who came to Jason's house to take him. Fortunately, Paul, Silas, and Timothy were out at the time and, learning of what was happening, escaped to Berea, which was forty-five miles away. Jason was taken captive in their place and arraigned before the rulers of the city. The accusation was that Jason had entertained those who violated Roman law by claiming there is another king besides Caesar and that king is Jesus. That mob made a prophecy without knowing it by saying, "These that have turned the world upside down have come here also" (17:6, AP). Indeed, the gospel would in time revolutionize the entire Roman world. Jason was forced to put up bond against harboring the likes of Paul and Silas again.

The people in Berea were more open to the gospel than the people of Thessalonica. It was easier to reason with them, and many were converted, including prominent Greek women and men. However, their prominence did not shield Paul from danger; when accusers came from Thessalonica, they realized that Berea would be no different in its reaction against him than Thessalonica had been, so they spirited him away to Athens. Silas and Timothy stayed, however, in Berea until Paul sent for them.

Athens (17:16–34)

Paul was alone in Athens. Though he had never been there before, he seems to have been no stranger to the place. He handled himself adeptly with the Athenians, so well in fact that he seemed to be one of them. As was his custom, he started his evangelism with the Jews in their synagogue, but the real object of his mission seems to have been to the population as a whole. He went directly to the people, encountering them in the marketplace. In this regard, he recapitulated the teaching methods of Socrates, who made himself available to any who would listen to him and sought to teach the people through open discussion and disputation with them.

As Paul made his case in the agora, or marketplace, he attracted the attention of the philosophers who were present there. It was the custom of Athenian society to gather in the agora to listen to speeches by any persons who felt they had something to say and then to quiz them and often to debate them on the validity of their ideas. It seems that the Athenians were less interested in the truth than they were in hearing new ideas. In this regard Paul appealed to them, for he presented a strange god about whom they had never heard before and talked about a dead man who had arisen alive from his grave. They asked themselves, "What will this babbler say next?" (17:18, AP). A babbler to the Athenians was a ne'er-do-well who liked to talk and pick up whatever scraps of food and clothing he could find that people had cast off in public places. Babbler denoted the image of a bird pecking away at a scrap of bread.

But after they listened to Paul, he made a better impression on some of the philosophers, for they summoned him to the Areopagus to explain in full his doctrine to those assembled there. The word *Areopagus* means "Hill of Ares," the Greek god of war. His Latin name is Mars. Hence the Areopagus is called Mars' Hill as well (17:22). On this hill met the chief council of Athens, which served as a forum to appraise various opinions being given the people and also as a judicial body. It was as an elite group to sift and appraise his doctrine that Paul was brought before it.

The two schools of philosophical thought represented on this occasion were Epicureanism and Stoicism: the former, discounting reason and advancing pleasure through experience, or self-satisfaction at the highest and noblest human level, as the true impetus for living; and the latter, exalting human indifference, or submission to the exigencies of existence through rigid self-discipline, treating with sublime disregard good fortune and bad fortune alike. Paul rejected both schools of thought and offered in their place belief in and allegiance to the one true God, whose rewards extend beyond this present life.

Paul began his discourse on Mars' Hill with the observation that the Athenians had an altar erected to the unknown god. It is this unknown God in whose name Paul speaks to them. This God, who made everything that is, does not dwell in the small temples that we build; neither can this God be worshiped in idols made with our hands. Rather, it is in and through God that we live and move and have our very life and existence. We are basically all alike, since God has made of one blood all nations that dwell on the face of the earth. We are God's offspring, and we ought not to think of God in terms of gold and silver objects, which we have designed and made. God has overlooked our folly in times past but now calls on us to repent. God has set a time to judge us and the whole world in righteousness by One whom God has appointed as the judge and has given evidence of this by raising that man from the dead. Some mocked Paul over the resurrection, but others said they would reserve judgment until they had heard him again.

A woman, Damaris, and a man, Dionysius the Areopagite, believed, and so did others with them. They became the nucleus of the Athenian church.

Corinth (18:1–17)

Corinth was the last major city Paul visited on his Grecian itineration. If he had had trouble from the populace in Thessalonica and Berea, what might he have expected from the people in Corinth, for Corinth was one of the most disorderly and corrupt cities in the Roman Empire? It was situated on a narrow isthmus connecting Peloponnesus with the mainland of Greece. It was the center of commerce between Rome's Asiatic provinces and the city of Rome itself and all its provinces in the west. It was on the main highway of Greece connecting the north with the south and itself the focal point of the two. There was no city in Greece of as much commercial importance as Corinth, and it was the capital of the Roman province of Achaia. It was a larger and, except for Hellenistic culture and intellectual refinement, a more influential and important city than Athens itself. It was a cosmopolitan city made up of peoples from all over the Roman world, including the Jews, who had a sizable colony there.

Strange as it may seem, however, Paul had little trouble in Corinth, certainly not enough to be driven out as he had been from Thessalonica and Berea. And he was not imprisoned there, as he had been in Philippi. When he left, he left voluntarily, as he had from Athens. But whereas in Athens he had stayed only a short time, just long enough to become known in the agora and to make his classical apology on Mars' Hill, which gave him a few believers who became the nucleus of the Athenian church, he remained in Corinth for a year and a half. There he not only started a church but supervised its early development.

When Paul first arrived in Corinth, he had gone, as his custom was, to the synagogue to declare the gospel first to the Jews. A few of them and their Greek proselytes believed, but the majority were so hostile and blasphemous that Paul dusted the dust from his raiments and left the synagogue with this malediction: "Your blood be upon your own heads; I am clean. From now on I will go unto the gentiles" (18:6, AP). Silas and Timothy came from Macedonia and joined him in Corinth.

Paul struck up a friendship with a Jewish couple from

Pontus, Aquila and Priscilla, who had resided in Rome until Claudius had driven the Jews out. Their occupation was tentmaking, as was his. They gave him room and board at their home, together with an opening into their business, so that he was able to make a living as a tentmaker during his stay in Corinth.

Jewish rabbis did not receive compensation for their religious services in the first century; they worked at secular employment in addition to performing their sacred duties. Paul did the same, though he did accept voluntary gifts from his converts. Paul received no compensation whatever from the Corinthians for his services to them; but he did receive material gifts from his converts in Macedonia while he was in Corinth (2 Cor. 11:9), especially from the congregation he left at Philippi (Phil. 4:15). Whether this was enough for him to give up his secular employment in Corinth and devote full time to the gospel is dubious.

Perhaps he did receive enough because he moved from the house of Aquila and Priscilla into the house of Titius Justus, which was next door to the synagogue. This enabled him to proclaim the message in the very environs of those Jews who opposed him and to win as many of their prose-lytes as he could to the Christian faith as they went on the sabbath to the synagogue. Evidently, Titius Justus had been one of those proselytes whom Paul had converted and was now a prominent member of the Christian community, as were Aquila and Priscilla.

To be sure, the Jews tried to give him trouble, but they got nowhere with the Roman deputy Gallio, who considered their complaints against Paul groundless, based entirely on their own religious regulations and having no foundation in Roman law and totally irrelevant to the dispensing of justice. The Emperor Claudius had had the Jews deported from Rome because of their quarrelsomeness and troublemaking. There-fore, Gallio sent them away from his tribunal.

Paul had success in evangelizing some of the Jews. He

actually converted Crispus, the chief ruler of the synagogue, and all his household with him. When Gallio dismissed Paul's Jewish accusers, the Greeks from the streets took Sosthenes, who had succeeded Crispus as head of the synagogue, and gave him a good beating in Gallio's presence at the tribunal. Gallio did nothing to stop them.

Paul's success in Corinth is testimony to the fact that the right place for the church is in the midst of the wicked and ungodly. Though we do not learn this from Luke in Acts, we know from Paul's Corinthian letters how unruly, contentious, and at times even immoral the congregation at Corinth was and what heartache it caused its founder. The members had come out of such a corrupt and degenerate environment. They were, as Paul admitted, just babes in Christ. Nonetheless, Paul called them saints, and saints by the grace of God they were to become. Corinth became one of the greatest centers of Christianity in the ancient world.

The Return to Antioch (18:18–22)

The second missionary journey ended where it began, in Antioch. But Paul did not sail directly to Seleucia, the port of Antioch. Instead he sailed from Cenchreae, near Corinth, to Ephesus in order to drop Aquila and Priscilla off in that city. From there he sailed again, not to Seleucia, but to Caesarea on the Judean coast. That is because he wanted to observe one of the religious feasts in Jerusalem. Apparently in preparation for the feast, he temporarily took the vow of a Nazirite in Cenchreae, where he shaved his head and abstained entirely from wine and strong drink. If the vow of the Nazirite was not for life, as it was not in Paul's case, it could be abandoned only in Jerusalem at the Temple, where the person who had taken the vow could be relieved of its obligations. It was generally taken as an expression either of one's gratitude to God for some extraordinary benefit or of a petition to God to satisfy some need or confer some special blessing. In Paul's case it was probably an expression of gratitude to God for the success of his Grecian mission.

He tarried at Ephesus only long enough to explain the gospel to the Jews in their synagogue. They showed interest, and he promised to come again to them for a longer stay if God so willed. He felt compelled to keep the feast at Jerusalem.

Consequently, he sailed from Ephesus to Caesarea. All Luke says is that after landing, he went up ''and saluted the church'' (18:22). This statement is ambiguous. If we did not know what had gone on before, it might mean just the congregation in Caesarea. But since Paul left Ephesus in order to reach Jerusalem in time to keep the feast and since he had taken a vow that he could be released from only in Jerusalem, we realize that Luke means Paul went up from Caesarea to Jerusalem to salute the mother church—the church of the apostles.

After he had kept the feast and fulfilled his vow, he returned by land to Antioch. No doubt he inspired the church with an account of his mission, especially that part of it in Greece, and confirmed its members in their belief in and support of his mission to the gentiles.

CHAPTER SEVEN

THE THIRD MISSIONARY JOURNEY

Acts 18:23–21:14

THE THIRD MISSIONARY JOURNEY was Paul's last voluntary itineration throughout Asia Minor and Greece; like the other two, it was a journey that he, by the guidance of the Holy Spirit, planned and accomplished freely without major external restraints. His last journey would be as a prisoner, and its itinerary would be determined by the government of Rome.

The third missionary journey was the most extensive geographically of any of the three, and its duration was much longer than the other two had been. During this journey, Paul covered the territory he had traversed in Asia Minor and in Europe on the earlier missions and stopped and preached at several new places as well, mostly ports of call at islands in the Ionian Sea. He did not cover Cyprus, however. After his separation from Barnabas, he did not visit Cyprus.

The focal point of Paul's third missionary journey was Ephesus, the capital of the Roman province of Asia. He spent more time in this city than in any other in the course of his three missionary journeys. In fact, he stayed so long, it looked as if his itineration might end there and he would settle down in Ephesus and become its first bishop. But Paul was too much of a missionary for that. He could not be satisfied until he had preached in Rome itself (19:21). Yet from Luke's account in Acts, Ephesus and Corinth are Paul's crowning missionary and evangelistic achievements, and of the two, Ephesus seems to transcend Corinth. It is Paul's jewel in the East, while Corinth is his jewel in the West.

Apollos (18:23–28)

While Paul was visiting again the churches he had established in Galatia and Phrygia, a man named Apollos arrived in Ephesus. He was a native of Alexandria in Egypt. He was a Jew, however, for the Jewish colony in Alexandria was a large one. It was so large, in fact, that the Hebrew scripture had been translated by and for that community of Jews into Greek, since it had become so Hellenized that many Alexandrine Jews had forgotten or never learned the Hebrew language. The translation made in Alexandria is the famous Septuagint. Whether Apollos knew Hebrew or not, Luke does not say. Two things he did know, though, and he used both to great advantage. One was the Greek language, and the other was the Hebrew scripture.

Alexandria was famous for its schools of philosophy and oratory. The world-renowned philosopher Philo, himself a Jew, was a native of Alexandria, where he interpreted the scripture by means of the Stoic concept of Logos. John used to advantage this aspect of Philo's philosophy in his explication of the incarnation in the first chapter of his Gospel.

Apollos likely was well versed in philosophy, especially Philonic philosophy, since he, like Philo, was a Hellenized Jew. This would have enabled him to find rapport immediately with the Hellenistic Jews of Ephesus. Not only could he speak Greek fluently, but he was a spell-binding orator who knew the scripture thoroughly. In all probability he gave it a Philonic interpretation. Whatever interpretation he gave it, his enthusiasm, sincerity, and gift of oratory made him most effective with the people.

Evidently, he had at least a smattering of Christianity, though Luke says that he knew only the baptism of John the

Baptist. That means definitely that he had a conviction of the heinousness of sin and the need for repentance and reparation. It probably meant as well that he knew the name of Jesus and recognized him as the promised Messiah who had finally come, for John the Baptist had acknowledged him.

But it is obvious from Luke's account that Apollos had no access to apostolic preaching and had not been blessed with the fullness of the gospel with its gift of the Holy Spirit. In other words, he had not acquired a full understanding of faith and how by faith alone one receives the Lord Jesus Christ as one's Savior. Priscilla and her husband, Aquila, discerned this when they heard him speak in the synagogue. After his message, they took him aside and offered him full instruction in the Christian way. Apollos gladly received such instruction and through them understood more perfectly the gospel. It is clear that Paul had left in Priscilla and Aquila two disciples who could carry on his work.

Apollos readily qualified as a true proclaimer of the gospel of Jesus Christ, so much so that when he decided to go to Greece, the brethren in Ephesus provided him with letters of recommendation. Luke tells us that in Greece he confirmed those who already believed through his preaching and he convinced the Jews through his interpretation of the Hebrew scripture that Jesus of Nazareth was the Christ.

Paul's Successful Ministry in Ephesus (19:1–22)

After the departure of Apollos, Paul arrived in Ephesus. He came down to the city from the northeast where he had been working in Galatia and Phrygia.

On his arrival he found a small group of sincere people who adhered to the teaching of John the Baptist. They had been convicted of sin and had repented and had registered their penitence in an act of baptism. Paul asked them if they had received the Holy Spirit either in the course of or as a result of their baptism. They frankly admitted that they had never even heard of the Holy Spirit.

Paul, then, explained to them the meaning of the Christian life, which begins at baptism, and showed them that John the Baptist had intended his ministry to be only preliminary and preparatory. He came to prepare people to receive the Messiah, who was Jesus Christ. Consequently, his baptism to repentance was insufficient. It needed to be superseded by baptism indicating one's belief in and acceptance of Jesus Christ as Lord and Savior. This belief and acceptance is accompanied by the gift of the Holy Spirit.

These disciples of John the Baptist believed Paul's message. They accepted Jesus Christ as their personal Savior and were baptized in his name. As had Peter and John before him, Paul laid his hands on them and immediately they received the Holy Spirit, who came on them with power, enabling them to speak in tongues and even to prophesy.

These two gifts, namely, of tongues and of the inspiration to prophesy, must have been extraordinary gifts, for there is no indication in the New Testament that they always accompanied baptism. However, the gift of the Holy Spirit is in the New Testament the normal result of baptism, which every Christian should expect to receive. The fact that Paul laid hands on the heads of the baptized converts no doubt symbolized the descent of the Spirit into their lives, just as the Spirit had descended on the converted Samaritans whom Philip had baptized when Peter and John laid their hands on them (8:14–17).

That is why today the ordained minister lays hands on persons when they are confirmed and join the church. Baptism symbolizes their forgiveness and cleansing from sin. Confirmation symbolizes their full membership in the corporate body of Christ, a membership they have voluntarily assumed, and the fulfillment of Christ's promise to give the Holy Spirit to all who believe (John 14:16–26; 16:7–15).

Paul's baptism of these disciples of John the Baptist is

the only incident in the New Testament where persons who had been baptized once were baptized a second time. As a result of this, some persons advocate rebaptism. Baptists, for example, insist that persons who come into their church from another denomination that practices infant baptism or uses a form of baptism other than immersion be rebaptized. There are others, some among United Methodists, who contend that a person who has sinned away the benefits of his or her baptism and who has come to repentance and received the grace of Christ to live a new life should signify the same in an act of rebaptism. I have seen persons whom I baptized as infants ask their minister to baptize them again when they joined the church.

Does this incident in the book of Acts validate such acts of rebaptism? I think not, because these disciples of John whom Paul baptized had never received Christian baptism before. They had not been baptized in the name of Jesus until Paul baptized them in Ephesus. The only valid baptismal formula for Christians is in the name of the Father, and of the Son, and of the Holy Spirit, for that is the only formula Jesus gave for his followers to use on persons they won through evangelism who desired to become members of Christ's holy church (Matt. 28:19).

Paul began his public ministry in Ephesus in his usual manner by speaking to the Jews in their synagogue on the sabbath day. In fact, judging from his first experience with them when he stopped briefly in Ephesus on his way to Jerusalem at the close of his second missionary journey, he had every reason to anticipate a gracious and fruitful ministry among them (18:19–21). But such was not the case. To be sure, he had some success among them. However, those who opposed him were so bitter in their opposition that within only three months, he had to separate his followers from them and go to another place.

Similar events occurred wherever Paul went. He was called to be an apostle to the gentiles, and he was especially adept in winning them to the Christian faith. But he had little success with the Jews. They were not only indifferent to him and his message but hostile as well; he was constantly in danger when he tried to minister to them.

He set up headquarters in the school of a man named Tyrannus, about whom we know nothing. He was probably a philosopher—Stoic, Epicurean, Platonist, or the representative of another system of metaphysics—who had opened a school where he taught in Ephesus and gathered from the populace his own disciples. Since Paul spoke in the school daily, he probably rented from Tyrannus, who welcomed him as a foil to his own instruction. If not a philosopher, Tyrannus had to be a rhetorician. If that were the case, Paul offered no competition to him. Rather, his presence and popularity drew more students to Tyrannus's classes, so Paul became an asset to his school. I am inclined to this latter opinion because Paul stayed there for two years.

Since Ephesus was the capital of Asia, and people from all over that Roman province came there from time to time, the gospel through Paul's preaching was not limited to the citizens of Ephesus but spread throughout the entire region. The Roman province of Asia covered the middle section of the western seaboard of what is now Turkey. It was not synonymous with modern Asia Minor; it was only a small geographical segment of it. The region of Mysia in the province of Asia with the port of Troas was north of it. Lycia and Pamphylia were south of it along the coast, and Pisidia, Phrygia, and Galatia were beyond it in the east.

Paul's success was remarkable; people all around responded positively to his message. He performed miracles in their behalf. Indeed, pieces of his clothing were carried out to the sick and diseased who could not come to him; and when his clothing touched their bodies, they were cured.

This is the only incident in the New Testament where this type of healing is said to have occurred. To be sure, the woman with the menstrual bleeding was cured by just touching the hem of Jesus' garment (Luke 8:43–48), but Jesus was wearing the garment at the time and the woman was actually in his presence. In Paul's case, his clothing was sent to the sick in distant places. This is the origin of the belief that inanimate objects can convey miraculous power when they have been handled or just blessed by a saint or holy person. For example, Helena, the mother of the Emperor Constantine in the fourth century, claimed to verify her discovery of the cross on which Jesus had died by placing it against the bodies of sick people and watching, when she did so, their immediate recovery.

When the wandering Jewish exorcists try to improve their practice by calling on the name of Jesus preached by Paul to expel an evil spirit from a tormented man, the spirit answers by saying: "Jesus I know and Paul I know, but who are you?" (19:15, AP). With that retort, the man under the impulse of the evil spirit leaps on the exorcists and beats them so that they run naked out of the man's house. Evidently the man has stripped them of all their clothes in his struggle with them. Luke identifies these exorcists as the sons of Sceva, whom he calls a chief priest.

The magicians, sorcerers, and exorcists of the region were so frightened by Paul's powers, and yet convinced of the validity of his message, that they collected their books of magic and burned them publicly as they embraced the Christian faith. Paul wanted to go back to Greece, but his work in Ephesus was going too well to leave it. Therefore, he sent Timothy and a disciple of his named Erastus to Macedonia in his stead.

The Pagan Demonstration in Ephesus (19:23–41)

Paul might have stayed much longer than he did had not a demonstration against him and his work taken place that involved a sizable number of citizens. This arose in the silversmith guild, which made silver replicas of the statue of Diana in the temple to be sold to visitors to that sacred site from all over the Hellenistic world.

Ephesus was the center of the worship of Diana, or Artemis, as her Greek name was, in the entire Roman world. Diana was the goddess of hunting in Greek mythology. But her cult in Ephesus represented her as being far more than the goddess of the chase. Indeed, she personified to her worshipers the earth in its fertility and fruitfulness, for she had acquired the features of the Asiatic goddess, Cybele, or Mother Earth. Her image was that of a woman of many breasts; the golden statue in the temple represented her as such. That is what the silversmiths duplicated and sold in abundance to the pilgrims and tourists who came in large numbers to Ephesus all the year round.

Ephesus in itself was a splendid city, one of the most beautiful in the Graeco-Roman world. Its wide main thoroughfare, which could accommodate several chariots in a row as well as pedestrians, its inviting shops and invigorating public baths, its stadium and large theater, which would seat twenty thousand people, made it the Rome of the East. Add to all this its temple, which was the religious showplace of antiquity, comparable almost to the Parthenon of Athens. In fact, the Temple of Artemis, or Diana, was one of the Seven Wonders of the World. Whether people believed in Diana as a deity or not, they came to see her temple and to admire its artistry. Most of the Ephesians did believe in her divinity, and they looked on her as the protectress of their city and their very special deity.

The silversmiths had a vested interest in Diana, for most of their trade came from the purchase of her statue and other works of art that they made and sold in connection with her temple. One of them, Demetrius, organized his fellow silversmiths to resist Paul and to stage a demonstration against him. To reach the general public, however, and elicit the aid of the populace, they had to have a more attractive reason than their own financial welfare. They had to convince the citizens that Paul was preaching that gods and goddesses made with hands were only idols and that those he converted despised Diana and her temple. If his movement were allowed to spread, it would greatly diminish the influx of pilgrims and tourists into Ephesus, and the great temple for which Ephesus was noted might lose so much support that it would fall into disrepair.

If Demetrius and his cohorts had focused on the danger of bankruptcy to them from Paul, the townsfolk might have disregarded them. What was it to them whether Demetrius went bankrupt or not? But for the city itself to be put in jeopardy and their own goddess Diana damaged would be a calamity so great that they ought to exert every effort to avert it. Demetrius threw the whole city into an uproar.

Paul was not in sight at the time. However, the demonstrating citizens did see two of his associates, Gaius and Aristarchus, who were from Macedonia. They apprehended and carried them to the theater, where the enraged multitude assembled to decide what form of action should be taken. The Asiarchs, that is, the chief persons of the province, who had come to respect Paul, cautioned him not to venture into the theater. A prominent Jew named Alexander was trying to explain to the assembly that Paul was not in favor with the Jewish leadership and therefore not to associate Paul with the Jews. But the crowd would not hear him simply because he was a Jew and Paul was a Jew also. Many people had joined the multitude, not knowing the reason for all the excitement. The people were becoming hysterical and getting out of control. For two hours they shouted until they were hoarse: "Great is Diana of the Ephesians" (19:34).

Finally the town clerk arrested their attention. He told them they had nothing to fear from anyone. The statue of Diana had dropped out of heaven from Jupiter into their midst. Her religion was too great for anyone to injure. Paul had operated in a quiet and unobtrusive manner. He had violated no laws. If the silversmiths felt he had in any way injured their business, they had the law courts in which to sue him and to make their case. He said that the ugly public demonstration was doing more harm to the reputation of Ephesus than Paul could ever do. Besides, with no better case against Paul than theirs was, they were endangering themselves with the Roman government. The best thing they could do would be to go home. And they did.

Paul's Last Missionary Journey as a Free Person (20:1–21:14)

And Paul went home, too, not to Tarsus, where he was born and reared, but to Jerusalem, where he had been educated as a Pharisee among the rabbis. Jerusalem had always been his spiritual home, now more than ever as the site of his mother church.

He took a roundabout way to get there, however. He had a premonition that once he arrived he might never be able to resume his missionary activity again. Before going to Ephesus on this third missionary journey, he had visited the churches he had founded in what is now Asia Minor. On leaving Ephesus, he wanted to visit one more time the churches he had founded in Greece. So after the town clerk had quelled the uproar against him in Ephesus, he bade his Ephesian congregation good-bye and sailed away to Macedonia, covering all the churches in that province. Then, he went down to the province of Achaia, which includes the cities of Athens and Corinth, where he preached and worked as chief pastor and founding father for three months.

Luke in Acts tells us nothing whatever about Paul's constructive ministry in either Macedonia or Achaia. We have to put together as best we can the details from his Corinthian correspondence and his letters to the Thessalonians and a reference in Romans (15:19). Factions, disagreements, and open immorality had troubled the Corinthian church since Paul had left it, and even the validity of his ministry was in question there. So he had sent Titus ahead of him to Corinth to test the waters and report back to him. This Titus did and met Paul with a favorable report in Macedonia. Paul sent him, accompanied by two others, back again to take a collection among the Corinthians for the mother church in Jerusalem (1 Cor. 8:16–24). After that, Paul went to that troubled church. All Luke tells us is that Paul planned to sail from Achaia directly to Syria, but changed his route when he learned that the Jews had fomented a plot against him. Consequently, he left the province of Achaia and returned to Macedonia.

Luke lists seven persons whom Paul took along as traveling companions as he made his way back into Asia. He tells us where six of the seven came from: one from Berea, two from Thessalonica, one from Derbe, and two from the province of Asia, presumably Ephesus. He does not tell us where Timothy is from, because we already know from an earlier passage (16:1–2).

Some commentators have suggested that these seven were sent with Paul by their respective churches to present the collection their church had raised for the mother church in Jerusalem. This suggestion does not seem feasible to me. No one from Philippi or Corinth is mentioned in the list, and two names found there are from Galatia, which probably did not participate in the offering, for it had been several years since Paul had traveled through Galatia. It would have been foolish for the churches in Lystra and Derbe to send money from Asia Minor to Europe and then back again in order for it to reach Jerusalem.

The most reasonable explanation for this list of seven would be that these people were free at the time to travel with Paul and that they wanted to be with him in Jerusalem to testify to the success of his mission in their part of the world. The way Luke injects them into his narrative without any explanation is odd indeed.

Paul sent them ahead of him to Troas in Mysia on the continent of Asia. Paul follows after them to Troas, where he stays for seven days. His last stop in Macedonia had been Philippi. It was at Philippi on the second missionary journey that the "we passage" in Acts had ended, indicating that Paul had left Luke there when he went on to Thessalonica. Now the "we passage" begins again. This means that Luke had accompanied Paul from Troas to Philippi and had stayed there without Paul for more than three years.

Before sailing for Troas, Paul had kept at Philippi the Feast of the Unleavened Bread, which is a seven-day observance following immediately after Passover, a one-day observance. Its purpose is to give thanksgiving to God for the harvest and to consecrate the first-born of man and beast to God as well as to signalize the redemption of the first-born males of the Jewish people. During the eight days of Passover and Unleavened Bread, Jews are expected to abstain from eating any bread made with leaven.

Paul met on the first day of the week with the members of the Christian congregation at Troas and broke bread with them. This meal was a recapitulation of the Last Supper of Jesus and his disciples. In the early church this celebration generally included more than just bread and wine, though in the course of the meal this act of Jesus was repeated as the principal act in table fellowship. Paul also preached to the congregation. This is the first instance in the New Testament where it is noted that the Christian congregation observes the first day of the week, not the Jewish sabbath on the seventh day, as its day of worship. The first day of the week is the day on which Jesus rose from the dead.

The service must have been in the evening, however, since Luke tells us that Paul preached until midnight. The room where he preached was on the third floor of a building, brightly lit with oil lamps. Eutychus, just a lad probably in his middle or late teens, fell sound asleep under Paul's preaching. Since Eutychus was sitting on the ledge of an open window, he fell out and was killed. Paul went down, stretched out over his body, and restored him to life. I wonder if Eutychus apologized to Paul for going to sleep on him.

On the morning of the second day of the week, Luke and Paul's other companions sailed to Assos, but Paul chose to hike overland since the distance was only twenty miles. He joined the others there and sailed with them to Miletus. Their voyage from Assos to Miletus took them down the coast by Mitylene and through the straits between the Asiatic coast and the island of Chios down to the island of Samos, where they stopped at Trogylium for a day, and back to the mainland, where they disembarked at Miletus. They stayed at that city long enough for Paul to send to Ephesus (only forty miles away) and invite the elders of the Ephesian church to come to him in Miletus. There Paul delivered his valedictory address to the elders whom he had appointed to watch over and lead the church he had left in Ephesus.

The principal points Paul made in that address are (1) to recall to their minds the character and quality of his ministry to them; (2) to remind them of the trouble the Jews gave him and the anxiety and suffering he underwent in their behalf; (3) to state that he preached repentance and faith in Jesus Christ as the essence of the gospel; (4) to testify that he went now to Jerusalem not knowing what would happen to him there except that he knew by the Holy Spirit that afflictions awaited him; (5) to assure them that nothing concerned him, not even the loss of life itself, so long as he could testify to the grace of God in Jesus Christ; (6) to say that he had no regrets about his ministry to the people in Ephesus, for he was clean of the blood of all the people there, for he preached the full gospel to all of them; and (7) to admonish them to be diligent in their oversight of the Ephesian church and to feed the church of God there, which Christ purchased with his own blood.

Paul ended his discourse with a moving exhortation. He warned the elders of danger to them in the future and urged them to watch and pray. He told them that he sought nothing for himself. Like him, they, too, must support the weak and remember the words of Jesus: "It is more blessed to give than to receive" (see Luke 14:12). He said they shall not see his face anymore. He closed his message with prayer. The elders wept as they hugged and kissed him and said good-bye.

Paul and company put out to sea again. Their voyage carried them by Cos and Rhodes and into the Lycian port of Patara, where they changed ships, sailed within sight of Cyprus, and landed at Tyre, where the ship unloaded its cargo. That took seven days, during which time the Christians there pleaded with Paul not to proceed to Jerusalem. But when the ship was ready to sail, Paul and his companions were on board again. They stopped for a day at Ptolemais in order to encourage the Christians in that city. Finally they reached Caesarea, which was to be their point of disembarkation for Jerusalem.

In Caesarea Paul and his companions found hospitality in the home of Philip, one of the seven who had been made deacons by the Jerusalem church before the martyrdom of Stephen. It was he who had first won converts among the Samaritans and had baptized the Ethiopian eunuch. Because of his remarkable success in winning people to Christ, he had come to be known as Philip the evangelist. He had four virgin daughters who had the gift of prophecy.

However, Agabus was the one who foretold Paul's fate in Jerusalem. Just as he had done in Antioch, when he foretold the famine that would afflict the Roman world under Claudius Caesar and cause the church there to send relief by Paul and Barnabas to the mother church in Jerusalem (11:27–29), so now he came, this time to Caesarea, from Jerusalem to warn Paul not to go there. This time he made a demonstration of his message. He took Paul's girdle and put it around himself, binding his hands and feet with it, and said, speaking for the Holy Spirit, that the Jews in Jerusalem would bind the man that owned the girdle and would deliver him to the gentiles. His prediction was so graphic that Paul's traveling companions and his hosts in Caesarea besought Paul with tears not to go to Jerusalem. Paul asked them to refrain from crying, for they were breaking his heart. He was adamant. He was ready, not just to be bound, but also to die in Jerusalem for the name of the Lord Jesus.

Since Paul would not listen to their advice, all his friends could say was: "The will of the Lord be done" (21:14).

CHAPTER EIGHT

TOWARD THE ETERNAL CITY

Acts 21:15–28:31

ROME IS KNOWN as the eternal city. It was the capital of an empire that lasted a thousand years. For almost as long as the Christian era, it has been the seat of the papacy; and since the Council of Chalcedon in A.D. 451, its see has been the most powerful and influential of any see in Christendom. The pope has been, and is, the temporal and spiritual ruler of the largest church in the world. From the days of Constantine in the early fourth century, he has been the father of princes and the king of kings.

Paul lived too soon to have any relationships whatever to the papacy. Peter is reputed to have been the first pope. But if he were, he did not know it. The papacy as an institution did not exist in New Testament times. All the apostles, including Peter, were wandering evangelists. There is no evidence that Paul had any contact with Peter in the city of Rome.

Paul was a Roman citizen, however. As such, he enjoyed all the rights and privileges of a free citizen of the largest and most powerful empire on the face of the earth. Its capital was the metropolis of the western world. And Paul longed to visit Rome because he wanted to have some part in the life of the Christian community flourishing there (Rom. 1:8–13). These last chapters of Acts deal with the circumstances that led to Paul's being taken to Rome and describe the events on his way there.

Paul's final destination was not Rome. Like Abraham,

the father of his race, "he looked for a city which hath foundations, whose builder and maker is God" (Heb. 11:10). These final chapters in Acts bring to a close all that Luke tells us of Paul's evangelistic and missionary career. Luke does not tell us of Paul's death. But more important than Paul's being temporarily the prisoner of Caesar, he was after his conversion permanently the prisoner of Christ. The city of Rome was but his gateway into God's everlasting kingdom beyond the years. On his way to Rome, he saw before him the crown of righteousness that was laid up for him and that the Lord would give him on the last day (2 Tim. 4:8).

Jerusalem (21:15–23:35)

Paul's company was enlarged by people from Caesarea who desired to accompany him to Jerusalem for the celebration of Pentecost. Among them was a Cypriot named Mnason, who owned a home in Jerusalem and who invited Paul to be his guest in that city. Perhaps he had been converted by Paul and Barnabas on the first missionary journey. Their luggage was heavy, so they employed carriages for the sixty-four mile trip from Caesarea to Jerusalem.

On arrival, Paul met with the brethren in general and went the next day to give his report to James, the brother of Jesus, and the elders of the Jerusalem church. They received Paul's glowing report of his missionary successes with joy and thankfulness, but they reported to Paul the rumors about him in Jerusalem, namely, that he had treated Jews as gentiles and freed them from all requirements of the Mosaic law, including the rite of circumcising their male babies. As a result, thousands of converted Jews in the city were scandalized. Therefore, Paul had to declare in some graphic way that the rumors were false and that he had freed only gentile converts from the Mosaic requirements but had insisted on

Jewish Christians living up to the law that he had diligently kept.

James and the elders proposed that Paul defray the Temple expenses of four men who had taken the Nazirite vow and go into the Temple with them and join them in their ritualistic purification. This ceremony, begun on one day, could not be concluded until seven days later. Paul began the ritualistic process the day after the suggestion had been made to him. He thereby announced that his purification, along with that of the four men, would be finished seven days later. They would make their sacrifices together, and Paul would pay for all of them.

Some scholars have felt that this could not have happened and that Luke is in error here. They think making such a sacrifice to please the Jewish Christians would be a compromise too great for the apostle to the gentiles to make. He preached Christ who alone is the propitiation for all our sins. But that same Paul confessed he could be all things to all people if by any means he might save some (1 Cor. 9:22). He was willing to be to the Jews a Jew, that is, to live under the law for the sake of those living under the law, and to the gentiles, a gentile. He realized of course that he had been liberated from the bondage of the law and lived entirely by the grace of God in Christ Jesus. Thus, his willingness to perform the necessary purification rites by making a sacrifice in the Temple was for the sake of others. He did not want to hinder the progress of the newly converted Jews in the Christian faith. F. F. Bruce puts the matter succinctly when he writes, "A truly emancipated spirit such as Paul's is not in bondage to its own emancipation."

James and the elders did not give Paul good advice, however. It may have convinced the Jewish Christians in Jerusalem who were bound to the Mosaic law that Paul had never transgressed that law and was in full harmony with them. But it exposed him in the Temple to the unconverted Jews in the city. There were at the Feast of Pentecost some hostile Jews from Asia, probably from Ephesus itself. They had seen Paul in the streets with Trophimus, one of his gentile converts from Ephesus. No doubt Trophimus followed him into the Court of the Gentiles in the Temple area. There was a sign in the doorway between this court and the Court of Women, stating that any foreigner who passed over from the Court of the Gentiles into the Temple area proper would have only himself to blame for his subsequent death. Jews killed any gentiles who defiled their Temple with their unholy presence. These Asian Jews spread the false rumor through the crowd that Paul had admitted Trophimus into the sacred precinct of the Temple.

Consequently when Paul had done his sacrifice on the seventh day, as they espied him in the Temple, the Asian Jews let out a cry: "Men of Israel, help! Here is the man who speaks everywhere against the Jewish people, their law, and their Temple. Here is he who polluted this holy place by bringing Greeks into it" (21:28, AP). Since there were many men in the Temple area, this was enough to incite them and turn them into a mob. They grabbed Paul and pulled him out of the Temple proper, and the keepers of the Temple shut the doors behind him.

Fortunately for Paul, the Antonia was located adjacent to the Temple. This was the Roman fortress in Jerusalem, and it held a garrison of 760 infantry and 240 cavalry, which made up an auxiliary Roman cohort. Flights of stairs led down from the Antonia into the Court of the Gentiles. The fortress was built above the Temple and higher than any other building in Jerusalem so that the Romans could keep constant watch over the population.

When the Romans saw what was happening in the outer court of the Temple, the military tribune in command of the garrison rushed down with troops to stop the outbreak. If he had not, Paul would have been killed by the mob. When he tried to ascertain what Paul had done to cause such an uproar, everyone was too excited to give him an answer. Some people shouted one thing and some another. Most of them did not know what Paul was supposed to have done. Like sheep following one another, they had just joined in with the rest to do their part in doing what needed to be done by all loyal Jews who loved their Temple. The Romans arrested Paul at the scene and bound him with two chains. Then the soldiers lifted him bodily out of the crowd and carried him up the stairs toward the entrance to the Antonia.

Paul surprised the tribune by addressing him in Greek, the international language of the time. "Why, you speak Greek," the officer said. "I thought you were that Egyptian who staged a riot here not long ago and escaped with his murderous gang into the wilderness" (21:37–38, AP). The reference is no doubt to an alleged prophet of Egyptian origin who led, according to Josephus, a mob of Zealots to the Mount of Olives and assailed the city of Jerusalem to rid it of the Romans. Most of the assailants were hunted down and killed by the Roman governor Felix, but the Egyptian leader had escaped. There is a difference in the number of assailants given by the tribune and by Josephus. The tribune says there were only four thousand of them. This is probably correct, since the revolt was not a major one and was easily put down. Evidently Paul's appearance was such that the Roman officer thought he was an ignorant brigand, but Paul informed him that he was a citizen of Tarsus. And his tone of voice and use of Greek were such that the officer realized Paul was more than ordinary and let him speak.

When Paul addressed the mob in Hebrew, they immediately became an audience, for silence fell. He was able to make his testimony by recounting his own experience in which he was led to accept Jesus Christ as his Savior. It is similar to the account Luke gave when he described its occurrence, with a few details Paul now added. For example, he recalled it was high noon when the experience took place, and the heavenly light was strong enough to outshine the noonday sun. He referred to Jesus as Jesus of Nazareth, so there would be no mistake on the part of his audience as to who his Savior really was. They knew Jesus of Nazareth had been crucified. He added incidentally that his companions also saw the light but did not hear the voice so that they became afraid. Paul made the point with them that Ananias, who was the instrument of God in the restoration of his sight in Damascus and who had baptized him and told him to witness to Jesus Christ, was a strict adherent of the Mosaic law and was highly respected by the Jews. Paul reported that he came back to Jerusalem and prayed in the Temple. Indeed, it was in the Temple that God revealed to him that he should leave Jerusalem for his own safety. The fact that he had beaten and imprisoned Christians and had concurred in the death of Stephen would not now stand him in good stead with the Jerusalem Jews. He must go, God told him, to witness to the gentiles.

The crowd had heard him without interruption up to this point. But at the mention of the gentiles, they broke out in fury, casting off their clothes and throwing dust in the air, and demanded Paul's death. The officer ordered him to be taken into the barracks and questioned by scourging in order to get the truth out of him as to what he had really done to cause such an outbreak. Scourging meant being beaten with a whip impregnated with pieces of sharp metal, which lacerated the body.

At this point Paul identified himself as a Roman citizen, for the law forbade such punishment of a Roman. The centurion was amazed when Paul told him this, and he informed his superior that they had more on their hands than they realized. The tribune countermanded his orders, observing to Paul that he had bought his Roman citizenship and implying that it was no longer the honor it used to be, since most anyone could get it who was willing and able to pay a bribe. Paul responded, "You may have gotten your citizenship that way, but I was born a Roman citizen" (22:28, AP).

The chief officer now realized Paul was a person of prominence, and he became afraid because he had had him bound.

The tribune summoned the members of the Sanhedrin to the Antonia. He wanted to ascertain from them the crime, if any, of which Paul was guilty. The high priest at the time was Ananias (A.D. 47–58), an unworthy and disreputable man, who had been once accused of treachery but acquitted for lack of evidence; he was eventually deposed.

When Paul assured the Sanhedrin that he had lived in good conscience before God, the high priest ordered the man nearest to Paul to strike him in the mouth to indicate he thought Paul was a liar. Paul said in outrage to the high priest, "God will strike you, you hypocrite, for pretending to judge me by the law and yet behaving toward me contrary to the law" (23:3, AP). The Jewish leaders were scandalized by Paul's remark and cried out against him that he had then and there violated the law forbidding anyone to speak evil of God's high priest (Exod. 22:28).

Paul admitted he had broken the law but added he had not realized this man was the high priest. He had to have known who he was, however, due to his leadership in the interrogation. What Paul meant was that he could not believe God's high priest would conduct a hearing in a rough and violent manner contrary to the law (Lev. 19:15). Paul was being sarcastic; he knew very well to whom he was speaking.

The Sanhedrin was composed of Sadducees and Pharisees, the former adhering only to the Pentateuch and denying the resurrection, the latter accepting the historical and wisdom literature plus the prophets and using the commentaries on the law by their scribes. The Pharisees believed in the resurrection of the dead. Paul announced to the Sanhedrin that he was a Pharisee, and he very cleverly turned the tables on his opponents by saying that he was being indicted for declaring his hope in the resurrection of the dead.

His remark divided the Sanhedrin. The less powerful members of the body, the scribes, who were Pharisees, supported Paul against the chief priests, who were Sadducees. The former found no evil in Paul and said that it was possible an angel had been using Paul as his mouthpiece and that the assembly dare not fight against God. The two parties in the Sanhedrin could fight against each other, however, and that is exactly what they started to do. The Roman officer had to have Paul removed from their midst. That night the Lord Jesus appeared to Paul and encouraged him by commending him on his witness in Jerusalem and promising him that he would testify to him in Rome.

Outside, a party of more than forty Jewish fanatics covenanted together that they would neither eat nor drink until they had killed Paul. To accomplish this, they appealed to the chief priests to request a second hearing from Paul. It was contrary to law for the Sanhedrin to engage in a plot of this type, but in desperation people are not always too careful to observe the niceties of the law. Paul's sister resided in Jerusalem, and her son heard of the plot and told his uncle of it. Roman prisons were always open to relatives of inmates. Paul sent his nephew with a centurion to apprise the commanding officer of the plot.

While the tribune was listening to the lad's report, he made up his mind to get Paul out of Jerusalem immediately and to refer his case to the Roman procurator of Judea, who resided in Caesarea. To this end, he composed a letter to the procurator, giving him an account of what had happened, and sent Paul under the cover of darkness with a military escort of two hundred foot soldiers, two hundred spearmen, and seventy cavalrymen on the way to Caesarea. By forced marching, the party reached Antipatris, a distance of thirty-seven miles, overnight. The spearmen and the infantry returned to their barracks the next day; the cavalry transported Paul the twenty-five remaining miles to Caesarea where the governor received him and placed him in Herod's judgment hall.

Caesarea (24:1–26:32)

Felix, the procurator, or governor as we would say, was an unusual character. He had risen to prominence by his own bootstraps. Felix had been a slave and had not only achieved freedom and Roman citizenship but also this high position in the government of the empire. His brother had been a companion of two emperors, Claudius and Nero, but only in their debauchery. Felix was married to the Jewish princess, Drusilla; she was the daughter of Herod Agrippa I, who had jailed Peter and had been stricken at Caesarea and died shortly thereafter (12:22–23). Drusilla was Felix's third wife.

Five days after Paul's arrival in Caesarea, Felix heard his case at a formal trial where the high priest Ananias and the elders presented their charges against him. They did this through a regular trial lawyer, Tertullus, who, judging from his name, must have been a Roman practicing law in Judea. The charges were four: (1) Paul was a public nuisance—"a pestilent fellow" (24:5); (2) he had caused a riot in the Temple area and was an instigator of sedition; (3) he had caused sedition among the Jews throughout the Roman world, for he was "a ringleader of the sect of the Nazarenes" (24:5); and (4) he was making an attempt to profane the Temple.

Tertullus's use of "sect of the Nazarenes" is the first and only use of "Nazarenes" to indicate Christians in the entire New Testament. Jesus of course is called "the Nazarene," but not his followers, at least in the New Testament. Later a Jewish Christian sect by that name emerged in church history, but Tertullus's designation does not apply to them, for they acquired their name and organization after Paul's time.

Paul in his own defense made two points: first, that his accusers, the Jews from Asia, were not present as witnesses to testify against him; and, second, that the real issue in the case was that he believed and taught the resurrection of the dead.

Felix postponed his decision on the ground that he

needed to talk directly with Lysias, the military tribune in Jerusalem, who was not present. Meanwhile he put Paul in the custody of a centurion and allowed him free intercourse with his friends, the Roman equivalent of our behavior toward a person on bail awaiting trial. Felix brought his Jewish wife to converse with Paul and allowed him to testify again in her presence. On this occasion Paul's testimony was so convincing, especially as he spoke about righteousness and the judgment to come, that Felix trembled and told Paul at a more convenient time he would hear him again on this matter.

It is confusing really as to what Luke means at this point. Does he mean to imply that Felix was about to be converted to Christianity? That is the obvious meaning of the sentence. But what follows casts doubt on this interpretation. Luke says that Felix hoped to get a bribe out of Paul, so he talked with him off and on during his period of custody. He makes no further mention of a favorable disposition on Felix's part toward the gospel. Luke does tell us that before Paul's trial Felix had a rather thorough knowledge of "the way," meaning the Christian way to salvation.

Felix procrastinated in making a decision on Paul's case. He let it drag on until the end of his procuratorship two years later. He tried for his bribe to the very end, confirming the Roman historian Tacitus's appraisal of him: Felix "exercised the power of a king with the mind of a slave."

He was replaced by Festus, a more honorable person who tried to dispense justice in the cases tried. However, his stay in office was relatively short, for he died not many years after taking up his duties in Caesarea. Paul's case was the first one on his docket. Indeed, when he made his first courtesy visit to the Jewish leadership in Jerusalem, the chief priests called to his attention Paul's case and asked that it be tried in Jerusalem, for they intended that the original plot to kill Paul be carried out. Festus was too smart to be taken in by them so soon after his investiture as Roman procurator.

Obviously he had not heard of the case before, so he invited them to come with their testimony immediately on his return to Caesarea.

Festus had been governor only a fortnight when he sat in judgment on Paul's case. The Jews brought out all their old complaints against Paul, but they could not produce a shred of evidence to support what they said. Yet the fact that they were so vehement in their attack on Paul led Festus to assume that there was more to the case than met the eye. Perhaps it would be better to hear it in Jerusalem after all. He could gather more witnesses and also have access to advisors knowledgeable in Jewish beliefs and customs.

Paul had answered the charges the Jews brought against him in Caesarea and had declared that he had not transgressed Jewish law or in any way profaned the Temple, neither had he done anything detrimental to the reign of Caesar. Still Festus was hesitant to exonerate Paul lest later he should prove to be a revolutionary and a threat to the peace of the province. So he said to Paul, "Will you go back with me to Jerusalem and let us hear your case in the very city where your crime is alleged to have taken place?" (25:9, AP).

This alarmed the apostle. Jerusalem was the last place on earth he could expect to receive justice. So now he took advantage of his Roman citizenship and appealed his case to Caesar. There was nothing more Festus could do but acquiesce: "You have appealed to Caesar. To Caesar you shall go!" (25:12, AP).

Shortly thereafter Festus received a state visit from King Agrippa II, the son of Agrippa I and the brother or half-brother of Felix's wife, Drusilla. King Agrippa was accompanied by another sister, Bernice, rumored to be his mistress. Agrippa ruled certain territories in the north of Judea toward Syria, and Rome had accorded him the title of king. He was a Jew and was well versed in his Jewish religion. Festus, who hardly knew what to write about Paul in his report to Caesar, was glad of the opportunity to consult Agrippa in the matter.

When he apprised Agrippa of the case, Agrippa asked that he might see and hear Paul in person. Consequently a state gathering was arranged for the very next day. King Agrippa and Bernice entered the state chamber in pomp and splendor as did their host Festus. The military officers and principal citizens of Caesarea were present as well, for Festus had commanded them to come.

Paul's defense before King Agrippa was really a testimony, for he reviewed once again the remarkable experience he had on the road to Damascus, both the events leading up to it and its result in the mission God gave him to the gentiles. Paul's account to Agrippa was abbreviated. He told the king that he stood under accusation by the Jewish leaders because of his hope in the resurrection, which ought to be their hope as well. "If God is what we Jews believe God to be, why is it incredible that God should raise the dead?" (26:8, AP). This is what the Christians claim for Jesus of Nazareth, and Paul admitted he rejected this claim and did all in his power to persecute and destroy those who made it. But the living Jesus intervened and changed his mind on the road to Damascus.

In his narration of this experience, there are a few differences in detail from what Paul said to the crowd in Jerusalem. For example, he recalled that his companions, as well as he, were struck to the ground by the heavenly light, but he did not mention his blindness and its cure. He supplied no factual details about himself and his work except to say in general that in that experience Jesus Christ made him a minister and a witness to free people from the power of Satan and to give them their inheritance with the saints. He also recalled that Jesus said to him, "It is hard for thee to kick against the pricks" (26:14), which he had not recounted to the Jews in Jerusalem. This was a Greek saying, meaning, You cannot resist fate, which Festus and Agrippa were familiar with, but which would have meant nothing to the crowd at Jerusalem. There is no contradiction whatever in the two accounts. Like any of the rest of us, Paul recounted some things in one that he left out in another. He used what he thought was relevant to those he was addressing. The force of all that he said was that he had not been disobedient to that heavenly vision.

Festus had no comprehension of what Paul was saying. To that practical Roman, Paul appeared to be crazy. He realized Paul was a learned man, too learned in fact for his own good. He interrupted to say in substance, "All those books you have read, Paul, have made you raving mad. Nothing you have said here makes any sense" (26:24, AP).

But Paul saw that Agrippa was listening and weighing his words carefully. On the basis of Old Testament prophecies of the coming Messiah, he was trying to convince Agrippa that Jesus fulfilled them to the letter and that it was neces sary for him to suffer and as a result to be the first person to rise from the dead. (Others, like Lazarus, may have been raised from the dead, but Jesus was the first to rise from the dead by his own divine power.)

Paul said confidently to Festus that King Agrippa knew all the things he was talking about. To which King Agrippa replied, "Almost thou persuadest me to become a Christian" (26:28). We take this to mean that Paul almost converted Agrippa as a result of his testimony. That is what John and Charles Wesley thought. Charles preached a sermon entitled "The Almost Christian" on this text, and John used Charles's sermon and preached it often as his own; at least he included it in his published sermons.

But I doubt that this is what Agrippa really meant. About all he meant was that he realized Paul was trying to bring him on the basis of what he knew from the prophets about the Messiah to believe that Jesus of Nazareth was that Messiah. Agrippa was not prepared to go that far. His answer to Paul was probably no more than this: "Paul, do you think in these few words you have spoken to us today that you can make a Christian out of me?" To Agrippa, Paul replied, "I wish to God that you and all who hear me this day would become just as I am without my impediment of being a prisoner awaiting trial'' (26:29, AP).

When Festus and King Agrippa had retired from the state chamber to discuss Paul's case privately, the king assured Festus that Paul had done nothing in violation of the Jewish law, and Festus knew that he had not violated any Roman law. Both men realized Paul was guiltless. They shook their heads and said that Paul could have been set free and sent on his way to do what he felt compelled to do if he had not made an appeal as a Roman citizen to Caesar. Though the emperor would have no doubt been relieved not to have to hear Paul's case, Festus had no option but to send Paul to Rome since his appeal was a matter of public record.

The Voyage (27:1–28:13)

Paul was sent to Rome in the custody of a centurion, that is, a minor officer in the Roman army who had command of a century, or a group of one hundred soldiers. A Roman centurion would be the equivalent of a second lieutenant in the U.S. Army. The man's name was Julius of the Augustus band, or cohort, which was one of ten divisions of a Roman legion. A cohort numbered between three hundred and six hundred soldiers. The Augustus cohort was probably stationed not too far from Caesarea in Galilee, a part of the kingdom of Herod Agrippa II.

It is likely that Julius took only a few, perhaps six to a dozen, of his troops with him, just enough to guard his prisoners, indeed to kill them if necessary. Not many people could merit an appeal to Caesar. Aristarchus of Thessalonica is mentioned as a fellow passenger, and we might assume he was just another passenger on his way back from Judea to Macedonia except for the fact that Paul mentions in one of his letters that Aristarchus was a fellow prisoner in Rome.

Evidently he, too, was on his way to trial (Col. 4:10). Since the voyage falls under one of the "we passages," we know that Luke was accompanying Paul, though not as a prisoner. The transportation used was regular commercial travel. Fortunately for Paul, at the very outset Julius liked him and treated him with admiration and respect.

The journey to Italy was not by direct travel. Passengers would book a passage as far as a ship was going in their direction, disembark, and pick up another vessel as soon as one was available. The boats carried cargo as well as people. The first vessel used was a ship out of Adramyttium, a port on the northwest coast near Troas, which was sailing back from the south and stopped to pick up passengers at Caesarea. It stopped at Sidon to unload and load cargo, and Julius graciously permitted Paul to visit with Christian friends there.

The route of the voyage was roughly the same as the route Paul had taken from Assos to Caesarea when he went to Jerusalem for Pentecost just two years and more before. The trip was in reverse order of course and not so extensive, for Paul and company got off at Myra in Lycia and took another ship out of Alexandria in Egypt, which had as its final destination Italy itself. It was a grain ship, hauling wheat from Egypt to Rome. The merchants who sold the grain often owned the ship that hauled it as well and would travel along with their cargo. They received special concessions from the imperial government, for grain from the provinces was essential to the populace of Rome.

Sailing across the Mediterranean was generally safe from the middle of May to early September. But from early November to early March it was so dangerous that voyages ceased altogether. The captain of the Alexandrine ship hoped to reach Italy before the bad weather had set in. Unfortunately winds were not favorable, and the ship had difficulty reaching Fair Havens, a harbor right in the middle of the southern coast of Crete. This was an open harbor, however, and therefore subject to storms on the Mediterranean Sea; the ships lacked the protection of arms of land around them.

There was another harbor on the same southern coast of Crete some distance to the west on the direct route to Italy. It was Phoenix, today's Phineka, and its harbor was well suited for the wintering of ships. The owner of the vessel insisted, in order to protect his cargo, that they leave Fair Havens and winter in Phoenix. The captain of the vessel felt they could make this other port in relative safety.

But Paul did not agree; he said to attempt it meant risking their lives as well as the cargo. Paul based his warning on the fact that the Jewish Feast of the Atonement was already past. It fell on the tenth day of the seventh month. The Jewish year was a lunar year, and dates varied from year to year depending on the position of the moon. The Day of Atonement in A.D. 59, the most likely year of the voyage, was as late as October 5. The weather had already gotten bad, for the ship had had difficulty proceeding further.

However, the centurion yielded to the wishes of the ship's owner and the advice of the captain. On the first fair day, when the south wind was blowing softly, they put out from port expecting to reach Phoenix safely. In good weather it was only a day's cruise from Fair Havens. The weather seemed to be fine, and they were taking every precaution by hugging the shore as they sailed. But the gentle south wind was short-lived. It was soon displaced by the tempestuous Euroclydon, formed by a meeting of winds from the north and the east. These winds coming down from the mountains of Crete above them were so strong that the sailors could not man the sails of the ship. To strive to do so would have meant that the sails would have been torn to shreds, so the crew had to let the ship drift with the winds.

As the ship drifted under the island of Cauda, twenty-three miles south of where they had hoped to land, they had to draw in the little lifeboat attached by ropes to the larger ship from behind to keep it from being dashed into their ship by the gales. Also they had to fortify their vessel by binding tight ropes or cables around its planks to hold them together in the storm. They used pulleys to undergird the ship to keep it from falling into the quicksands.

Leaving the protective shield of Cauda, which obviously had no harbor to serve them, they took to the high sea again, where after a day they had to lighten the ship by casting overboard some of the cargo. The third day they threw out the tackle of the ship. The tempest would not die down. For days they sailed, not knowing where they were because sun, moon, and stars were hidden from view, and these were the only means they had for determining their course. Consequently, they gave up all hope and were too distraught to eat.

The apostle Paul reassured them. He said that during the night the angel of God stood by him and told him that he would stand before Caesar in Rome and that God had given to him all those on board ship with him. He assured them that there would be no loss of life among them but that they would lose the ship.

After fourteen days, the sailors saw signs to indicate they were approaching land. They sounded for the depth of the sea. As the water got less and less deep, they stopped the ship and cast out four anchors lest the ship be dashed against the rocks. It was the middle of the night, and they waited anxiously for the morning light. The sailors got frightened, however, and started to abandon the ship and escape in the little lifeboat. They pretended to want to use the boat to cast anchors out of the bow of the ship. The other four anchors were out of the stern. Paul warned the centurion and the soldiers that unless the sailors remained with the ship none could be saved, so the soldiers cut the ropes and set the lifeboat adrift before the sailors could use it.

When daylight came, they saw that land was near and took heart again. Paul urged them to eat to gain strength, for he assured them that no one would be hurt. He took bread in his hands and broke it and gave thanks to God. Some commentators have insisted that in this act he celebrated the Lord's Supper with them. This is absurd. Except for him and Luke and Aristarchus, there were no Christians among them. The others would not have known what the Lord's Supper was all about. What Paul did was to say the table blessing, to give God thanks for their rescue and the provisions for an ordinary meal. They could all understand that and under those conditions appreciate Paul's prayer.

They saw a creek ahead, which they thought would make a good harbor for the ship. They threw out the rest of the wheat. Unfortunately this did little good, for as they sailed inland, the ship ran aground, its bow got stuck in the mud and sand, and its stern was broken to pieces by the waves. In keeping with their discipline, the soldiers started to kill the prisoners, lest they take the opportunity to escape. But the centurion, in order to save Paul, stopped them and ordered all who could to swim to land. Those who could not were to take pieces of the ship and float in. All reached the shore unhurt.

The people on shore kindled a fire and received the party hospitably. Because they could not speak Greek, Luke called them barbarians, but they were really civil and decent people. The name of their island was Melita, which is modern Malta. The Maltese proudly claim that their church was established by the Apostle Paul. Yet Luke provides us with no evidence to support this claim, such as evangelistic preaching by Paul on the island, his organizing a congregation, or the appointment of elders as we have seen him do in other places. But all these things can be taken for granted.

Paul gained immediate influence with the people. As he was placing wood on the fire the natives had built for him and his companions, an adder, or horned snake about two feet long, very venomous, crawled from the unignited wood onto Paul's arm and bit his hand. The apostle took no notice of the incident except to pry loose the reptile and throw it in the fire. But the natives took notice. At first they thought it was a sign that Paul had committed some horrible crime and was escaping execution as a criminal. Fate would not permit this. The gods had sent this adder to destroy him. They fixed their gaze on his hand. When it did not become swollen and he showed no signs of being poisoned, they changed their opinion and took him to be a god in human guise.

Paul's reputation, gained by this incident, went before him. The ruler of the island, Publius, entertained him and his fellow passengers for three days. Publius's father was ill of dysentery, and Paul cured him. People from all over the island came to Paul for relief, and he healed them, too. To do this, he had to pray over them.

It is unreasonable to think that he did not convert them as well. Paul knew that for a person to be whole, that person had to be right with God. He stayed three months on Malta. Therefore, the Maltese are no doubt correct in claiming that Paul won the entire population to Jesus Christ. When the shipwrecked passengers left, the people gave them all they needed for their trip and honored them, especially Paul, in every way they knew how.

It must have been a considerable time after the Feast of the Atonement, say a month or so, that the ship's crew had risked the cruise from Fair Havens to Phoenix; for after such an ordeal as they had been through, they would not have undertaken to sail again until spring of the next year. Then, they booked passage on another ship from Alexandria, which had wintered in Malta. On its way to Italy, it stopped for three days at Syracuse, the chief port of Sicily, called at Rhegium at the tip of the Italian boot, and after one day in port there, the gentle south wind enabled them to arrive safely in the harbor of Puteoli, which was their port of disembarkation. Their long voyage was over.

Rome (28:14–31)

Paul's destination was Rome. His purpose in being there was to stand trial at Caesar's judgment seat. He was met by the Christians at Puteoli with whom he stayed for a week. Obviously the centurion was most lenient. He had no definite time to arrive in Rome, so he adapted himself to Paul's desires and let him do pretty much what he wanted to do.

When the Roman Christians got news of Paul's arrival in Italy, they came out from the capital to the Forum of Appius and the Three Taverns to meet Paul and to escort him into Rome. The group that met Paul at the Forum of Appius had come a distance of forty-three miles; the second group, waiting at the Three Taverns for him, had come thirty-three miles. The Forum of Appius was about halfway between Puteoli and Rome, so in all probability the Christians of Puteoli went with Paul to the point where the first group from Rome met him.

Seeing all these brethren brought Paul great joy and gave him much courage. Together they took the Appian Way into Rome, and without being aware of it almost recapitulated their divine Lord's triumphal entry into Jerusalem.

The centurion fulfilled his mission by delivering his prisoners to the captain of the guard. Paul, then, was permitted to live in a house with only one soldier to guard him. This is what we would call house arrest. He was not permitted to wander throughout the city, though.

Consequently, after three days, he invited the Jewish leaders of Rome to visit him in his house. He explained to them why he was in Rome and indicated those in Jerusalem responsible for his predicament, all the while avowing his innocence of any crime against the Jewish nation. It is obvious that the Jewish leaders in Rome had received no information from Jerusalem about Paul and the nature of the complaints against him. In fact, they told him that people who had come from Judea to the capital had had nothing detrimental to say about him. The chances are that those people did not mention him one way or the other. They had heard about the Christian sect, however, and all reports of it had been bad, so now they wanted to hear about it from one of its own members.

They gave Paul time to prepare his apology, and on the day appointed, they came back with as many others who could conveniently accompany them. Paul took a whole day to talk with them about the kingdom of God, using both Moses and the prophets to persuade them to believe in Jesus Christ. Luke says some were persuaded and some were not. Evidently not enough were persuaded, or rather those who were persuaded were not persuaded enough to accept Christ as their Savior and be baptized. Paul dismissed them with the words of Isaiah, who said that the heart of the people has become obtuse, their ears dull, and their eyes closed, so that God can't heal them (Isa. 6:9–10). Paul told them as they left that, since they would not hear, he would preach to the gentiles, to whom God had sent the gospel. He knew they would be open to it.

As he had done everywhere else, so Paul did in Rome. He preached first to his own people, the Jews. But when they would not hear him, he preached to the gentiles, who did hear him. For two years he received as many as would come in his house and preached to them the kingdom of God and taught them about Jesus Christ. The Roman government put no restraint on him so long as he did it in his own house.

At this point the Acts of the Apostles closes. If Paul arrived in Rome in the spring of A.D. 60, based on the probable dating of the shipwreck in the winter of A.D. 59, which is consistent with general Pauline chronology, Acts ends in the spring of A.D. 62. Paul's hope had been fulfilled. He had come to the Christians in Rome, and he was gathering fruit among the gentiles there as he had in all the other places where he had been (Rom. 1:13). Though Paul did not plant the church in Rome (Peter had probably done that, or else it had come into existence by means of converted Jews of the Diaspora who had heard the apostles in Jerusalem and returned with the Christian faith to Rome), Paul now had become a powerful factor in its development and would give it impetus by his martyrdom some years later.

Luke had accompanied Paul to Rome. He had begun his association with him at Assos, when they sailed together to Macedonia. About three years later, he joined Paul again at Philippi, where Paul had left him, and traveled with him to Jerusalem, where Paul was arrested and transported to Caesarea to languish for two years in Roman custody. There Luke joined him again for his voyage to Italy. The intimate friendship with Paul and lengthy association gave Luke the opportunity to gain information about Paul's career, which he describes so vividly from the start in the book of Acts. He does not carry the account, however, to the point of Paul's martyrdom. Why, we do not know, and it would be idle to speculate about the reasons. Enough! He has shown us in fullness Paul the missionary and evangelist. And the subsequent history of Christianity has proved Paul to be the greatest missionary of all times.

QUESTIONS FOR REFLECTION AND STUDY

Introduction

1. Why do you think it has been important through the centuries to have Luke's history of the beginnings of organized Christianity?

2. Does it bother you that Luke may deliberately have presented New Testament Christianity in a flattering light? Does this possibility lead you to believe that Luke's account may be unreliable? Why or why not?

3. How do you account for the differences between events related in Acts and in Paul's Epistles? Are these differences important? Why or why not?

4. In what ways do you feel that the Acts can be justifiably called the Gospel of the Holy Spirit?

5. Luke evangelizes through his writing rather than preaching. Do you think both forms of evangelism are still effective today? Are they both necessary? Which form is most helpful to you personally? Why?

Chapter 1

1. Luke addresses the Acts of the Apostles to Theophilus, a name that means "dear to God." Whom do you consider

to be dear to God? In what ways do you feel that you are
dear to God?

2. In what ways are the meanings of *passion* in Acts and
passion in contemporary usage different? In what ways
are they similar? What is your understanding of the
passion of Christ?

3. During the forty days that Christ appeared to his disciples following his resurrection, he taught them about the
kingdom of God. However, he did not equate the kingdom of God with the church as we know it—as a
temporal organization. Instead, Christ was concerned
with the reign of God, both in heaven and on earth.
What is your understanding of the kingdom of God? What
roles does the church play in it? Does the church ever
conflict with the reign of God? When might that be true?

4. In what ways are we justified in considering the church
to be the kingdom of God on earth? In what ways is that
understanding in error?

5. Following Christ's resurrection, his disciples believed
that the restoration of the kingdom of Israel was immi-
nent. What difference might it have made in the development of the church if the disciples had known precisely
when the kingdom was to be restored? What difference
might it make in your own life if you knew when Christ
would return? What difference might it make in the life
of the church? Are these differences important?

6. Jesus told his followers that their sole mission on this
earth was to witness to him. They were to begin proclamation at home, then to their enemies, and then all over
the world. Is that mandate still valid for his followers
today? Who would be included if you proclaimed the
risen Christ at home? Who are your enemies? Is it
possible for you to proclaim Christ all over the world? In
what ways?

7. Consider Christ's mandate from the point of view of the
church. Who are those at home? her enemies? the whole

world? Does the church fulfill this mandate today? Why or why not?

8. When the disciples witnessed Christ's ascension, angels had to remind them to quit gazing at the sky when they had work to do on earth. Are contemporary Christians ever guilty of simply sky-gazing when there is work to be done? In what ways might this be true in your life? What "angels" call you back to the task at hand?

9. Do you believe in a literal interpretation of Christ ascending into heaven? Why or why not? Why do you think Christ's ascension was so important to the early church that it became an article of faith?

10. What are your personal beliefs about the second coming of Christ? Do you expect it to be a cataclysmic event?

11. The disciples believed that it was important to replace Judas. Do you agree or disagree? Does the method used in the selection of a replacement bother you? Do you believe that God was at work in choosing Matthias? Why or why not?

Chapter 2

1. What is your reaction to the statement, "Jesus did not establish the church"? Do you think he intended that an organized church be established, or might Jesus have had something different in mind?

2. How is the Holy Spirit the founder of the church?

3. Before the Christian community could be empowered by the Holy Spirit to carry on Christ's work, two requirements had to be met: they had to be of one mind, and they had to be gathered together in one place. These requirements were met at Pentecost in the upper room. Does the empowerment received by those disciples extend to Christians today? Can it be said that Christians are of a single mind, of one accord?

4. What divisiveness is found among contemporary Christians? What factions contribute to disunity? How does this impede the reign of God on earth?

5. Since the beginning, Christianity has been a social movement. What does this suggest about the importance of corporate worship? What effect, if any, does this understanding have on your spiritual life? What is the relationship between corporate and private worship for you?

6. The symbols of wind and fire are used to describe the movement of the Holy Spirit on Pentecost. How are these symbols meaningful to you?

7. The Holy Spirit was evident to the disciples in what they heard, what they saw, and what they felt. Give some examples of how the Holy Spirit is evident to you.

8. After the Spirit descended on the little band of followers, they went immediately into the streets to announce the good news of Jesus Christ. Understanding that people often mock what they do not understand, Peter effectively used the ridicule of the crowd as a lead-in for his sermon. How might you turn scoffing into effective evangelization?

9. Which characteristics of the New Testament community do we find in the church today? Which are different? Is it possible or even desirable for the church to operate in the same fashion now? What might be some obstacles?

10. What do you think it was about the early Christian community that found favor with the people and contributed to the steady flow of converts? What do you think might have a similar effect on people today?

Chapter 3

1. Why do you suppose Christian activity was confined at first to Jerusalem? Was it simply because of Christ's mandate, or may other factors have been involved?

2. Do we still experience miracles? How does Christ through the activity of the Holy Spirit perform miracles today? What miracles have you experienced in your life?

3. What afflicts people today? What are some of the ways in which we, too, make good use of our afflictions?

4. Do Christians make a display of their generosity to others? How do we make our alms evident?

5. The lame man, once healed, had no petitions to offer to God. Instead, he offered only prayers of thanks and praise. Think about your prayer life. How is it distributed with respect to petitions, thanks, and praise? How might it be improved?

6. After the healing of the lame man at the Beautiful Gate, Peter spoke to the crowd, giving credit for the miracle to the crucified and risen Christ. However, not stopping there, Peter immediately turned condemnation into hope and assurance for his listeners, evoking from them a response of faith. Can you give some examples of ways in which Christians have settled for condemnation, stopping short of the life-giving exhortation to faith in the risen Christ?

7. Peter discerned that Ananias had put his own interests before those of God and the Christian community and had yielded to the devil by lying. As a result, Ananias died. Does this imply either literally or figuratively that Christians place themselves in mortal danger by thinking of themselves first or by lying? In what way might this be true?

8. There has been much controversy over the only "unforgivable" sin. Based on the story of Ananias and Sapphira, describe your interpretation of what constitutes such sin.

9. The early church was not only a place of joyous fellowship and worship; it was also God's house of judgment. Is this characteristic of your church? Why or why not?

10. Gamaliel quieted the enraged Jewish assembly by pointing out that if the Christians were indeed fanatics, they

would eventually destroy themselves. And if they were of God, then there was nothing that could be done by the Sanhedrin to stop them. What contemporary examples can you cite in which this judgment has proven true?

11. The early Christians placed importance on administration within the community and considered it a vital part of their ministry. How does this compare with attitudes in your church toward administration?

12. How do you react to the fact that representatives of the group making the complaint to the congregation about unfair treatment of widows were the very ones chosen to oversee just distribution? How might this help resolve dissension in your church? in the church at large? What would your reaction have been if you had been one of those chosen? one of the others?

13. What implications for ministry can be drawn from the fact that both the first martyr (Stephen) and the first missionary (Philip) were members of the diaconate, not apostles?

Chapter 4

1. What do you think of the concept that God used persecution to spread the Christian faith?

2. Why do you think Stephen's martyrdom helped initiate evangelism outside Jewish territory? Might it just as well have taken place anyway?

3. What is the difference between magic and miracles? Do modern people ever confuse the two? In what ways?

4. Are Christians ever guilty of using their influence as Christians to better their positions in life or to further their own ends? What are some of the subtle ways in which they might do this? Have you ever used such influence? What was the result? How do you feel about it now?

5. Luke records a number of events in Acts that underscore the inclusiveness of the early church and the fact that no handicap, physical or otherwise, would exclude a person from full fellowship in the Christian faith. In what ways is that inclusiveness evident in your church? in the church at large? How is it not? What groups of people would feel excluded in your church? Whom might you personally consciously or unconsciously exclude?

6. Philip encountered the Ethiopian eunuch in a most unlikely place and converted him to Christianity. What are some of today's unlikely places in which you may encounter persons and invite them to faith in the risen Christ?

7. Three forms of baptism were likely in the early church: immersion, pouring, and sprinkling. By which method were you baptized? What is the significance of baptism in the life of a Christian, whatever the method?

8. Saul was a devout man and ardent in his faith. Nevertheless, in the name of that faith, he persecuted others. When have Christians been guilty of persecuting others in the name of their faith? Do you feel it is justified? Why or why not? Name several examples of ways in which modern Christians persecute others.

9. How do you resolve the differences in the three accounts of Saul's conversion as related in Acts? Are these differences important?

10. When the believers in Jerusalem doubted the sincerity of Paul's conversion, Barnabas gathered the facts and interceded with them on Paul's behalf. Do you think you would be willing to speak out before a hostile group in favor of a controversial person? Why or why not? What are some instances in which Christians might be called to do so today?

11. Paul believed that Christ called him to be an apostle in the same way in which he called the original twelve disciples. Why do you agree or disagree with him?

12. When Peter proclaimed the gospel to the Roman centuri-

on Cornelius, he effectively changed the policy of the early church, removing all distinctions among persons. Would it be possible, or even right, for a single person today to change the policy of an entire denomination? the church as the body of Christ? the policy in your church? How are policy changes likely to come about now?

13. What or whom do you consider "unclean" in modern society? How is that affected by the statement that nothing God has created is unclean?

14. How do you understand the statement that baptism does not produce regeneration? Why do you agree or disagree?

15. The author says that the prayers of the Christian community for Peter were answered although, judging by their surprise when he appeared at the door, they weren't sure they would be. Do you ever pray for something without really believing that your prayer will be answered? Does this affect the outcome of your prayer?

16. Do the statements that God used Herod's tyranny to release Peter for wider service and that God used the martyrdom of Stephen to evangelize the world trouble you? Why or why not?

Chapter 5

1. How might the gospel still spread "accidentally" today? In what ways do you spread it "accidentally"?

2. How is the gospel deliberately propagated today? Do you feel that the missionary imperative is as important today as it was to the early church? Which is more comfortable for you, spreading the gospel accidentally or deliberately, or are you equally comfortable with both? In what ways are the missionary efforts of the early church and those of the modern church different? In what ways are they similar?

3. According to Acts, how was the church at Antioch

charismatic? Is this what we understand as charismatic today? Name some similarities and some differences between the church at Antioch and your church. Are those similarities/differences important? Why or why not?

4. How does the contemporary church seek the guidance of the Holy Spirit? How do you? Who are the teachers and prophets in today's church? in your church? Are they as clearly recognizable as they were to the Antioch church? How do we know the teachers and prophets? Are we ever mistaken?

5. The laying on of hands is mentioned a number of times in Acts and through the scriptures as a whole. What meaning did this act symbolize for the early Christians? What meaning does it have for modern Christians? for you personally? Is it as prominent today as it was in the first century? Why do you think this is so?

6. At Cyprus, Paul apparently took over the leadership of the missionary enterprise from Barnabas, presumably with Barnabas's consent. What do you think your reaction would be if you were replaced as the head of an important task? How would your reaction be similar to or different from that of Barnabas?

7. John Mark, Barnabas's nephew, deserted the mission at Perga and returned to Jerusalem. Have you ever reluctantly taken part in church work? What was the result? Have you ever had to give up for some reason? How did you feel about it? How did others react to your decision? What did you learn from your experience?

8. If you were invited to speak to others on the scripture, with which portions would you be qualified or most comfortable? In what areas would you like to be more prepared?

9. Do you ever become jealous of those whose abilities seem to exceed yours? How do you usually relate to such people? What attitude do you think is most Christian?

10. In Iconium, the citizens were divided over the message

of Paul and Barnabas. In what areas or over what issues does Christianity divide people today?

11. The controversy over circumcision threatened to impede the spread of Christianity among the gentiles. Name some things that Christians hold tightly to today that might exclude others from Christian fellowship. What attitudes might exclude others in your church? What are some of your personal attitudes that might be exclusive?

12. The early Christians were careful to avoid causing offense to others needlessly. Are modern Christians as sensitive? In what areas might we need improvement?

13. When Barnabas insisted on allowing John Mark to participate in the second missionary journey, Paul and Barnabas parted company. Barnabas wanted to give John Mark a second chance. Paul's main concern was the success of the venture; he considered taking John Mark along to be risky. Which man do you think was right? Which attitude appears more Christian? What would you have done in this situation? How might you have felt if you were John Mark?

14. Acts relates that the Holy Spirit prevented Paul, Silas, and Timothy from carrying the gospel northward into Bithynia. How is the Holy Spirit's opposition made evident today? Has the Holy Spirit ever prevented you from doing something you had planned to do? How was this apparent to you?

Chapter 6

1. There is no indication in Acts that Paul sought the guidance of the Holy Spirit when he began his missionary journey into Europe. He seems to have assumed that it was God's will that he do so. Do you think that Paul was on shaky ground in making this assumption? Would you be comfortable in assuming that your action is God's

will? Under what circumstances might that be true for you?

2. Acts relates a number of instances in which God spoke to the apostles in a dream. For instance, in a dream a Macedonian asked Paul to come and help him and his people, and following a dream, Peter spread the gospel to the gentiles. Do you think that God still speaks to people through dreams? Have you ever experienced such a revelation?

3. The New Testament often tells of the conversion of a person along with the whole household, for example, Cornelius, Lydia, and the Philippian jailer. What do you suppose is meant by this? Does one person in the household make the decision for everyone, or is it an individual decision? Would this be likely to occur today? Why or why not?

4. Paul exorcised the demon from the young woman who told fortunes because he realized that her gift was actually a curse to her. What gifts do we encounter today that may in reality be a curse? Name some examples of ways in which we might use others for our profit and to their detriment.

5. In the case of the Philippian jailer, near personal disaster led to his conversion. Even today, times of personal crisis often lead to conversion or to a deepening of one's faith. Why do you think this is true? Does it ever have the opposite effect? What factors might contribute to these two different reactions?

6. We are told that in Thessalonica Paul worked in order to provide for his needs, refusing to accept handouts from those to whom he preached. Why do you suppose Paul did this? What are the implications of Paul's actions for today's church, both positive and negative?

7. In Athens, Paul went directly to the people in the marketplace and handled himself so adeptly that he seemed to be one of them. What does this say about the

role of an ambassador for Christ? What would be the marketplace for modern Christians?

8. The Athenians' first impression of Paul was that he was a babbler, a ne'er-do-well. After hearing him speak, some of them had a better opinion of him and wanted to learn more about his doctrine. Do you form snap first impressions of people? How accurate are they? Have you ever had to change your mind about someone after you had formed an opinion?

9. What is your reaction to the statement that the right place for the church is in the midst of the wicked and ungodly? How do you interpret this statement? Is this true for your church?

10. We know from Paul's letters that members of the congregation at Corinth were unruly, contentious, and at times even immoral, and yet Paul called them saints. How do you account for this? Do you agree or disagree with Paul?

11. Paul took the vow of a Nazirite in preparation for observing a religious feast in Jerusalem. He shaved his head and abstained from wine and strong drink. This vow was usually undertaken as an expression of either gratitude or petition to God. For what religious festivals do modern Christians prepare in special ways? What form do those preparations take? What forms of preparation for religious observances are meaningful to you personally?

Chapter 7

1. Paul stayed so long in Ephesus that it looked as if he would settle down there and become its first bishop. When our work is going well, are modern Christians ever tempted to settle back and enjoy it rather than to

move ahead? How do we know when it is time to move in another direction?

2. Apollos was uniquely gifted both by natural ability and by training to preach the gospel effectively. What natural abilities do you have that can enable you to reach people in the name of Christ? What training have you had that prepares you for this task? Which abilities do you think you need to develop in order to increase your effectiveness?

3. Although gifted, Apollos realized his shortcomings and was willing to accept the instruction of Priscilla and Aquila. Under whose instruction are you willing to place yourself in order to understand more perfectly the gospel?

4. What do you understand to be the difference between baptism and confirmation? Are both equally important? Is either of them optional? What does each mean to you personally?

5. Paul experienced much opposition in preaching the gospel. However, he seemed to know when to call it quits and turn to another area in order to win persons to Christ. Do you ever have difficulty knowing when to persevere and when to give up? Upon what criteria do you base your decision? Do circumstances alter your criteria?

6. Luke tells us that Paul performed miracles of healing and that even his clothing could cure persons who touched it. What is your reaction to the concept that inanimate objects that have been handled or blessed by a saint or holy person convey miraculous power?

7. The magicians, sorcerers, and exorcists at Ephesus were frightened of Paul's power, but were so convinced of his message that they accepted the Christian faith. As a symbol of that faith, they gathered and burned their magic books. What symbolic act would be meaningful to you personally as an expression of your faith? Can you name others that might be appropriate for modern Christians?

8. The members of the silversmith guild at Ephesus rejected

Paul's message of the gospel because it threatened their financial well-being. Do Christians ever reject certain aspects of the gospel when it interferes with material comfort? Are we ever guilty of picking and choosing those precepts of our faith that are most convenient? Name some examples of how this might be true.

9. When Paul made it known that he intended to travel to Jerusalem and that his journey would ultimately mean his death, his friends and followers implored him to change his mind. Have you ever had a difficult task to perform only to have your family or friends try to dissuade you? How did you handle the situation? Have you ever tried to convince others to change their mind? Do you think it is possible for well-meaning people to interfere with God's work in such a way?

Chapter 8

1. Paul spoke about being all things to all people in order that he might win some to Christ. When he was with Jews, he observed Jewish traditions; when he was with gentiles, he refrained from forcing Jewish beliefs on them. Does this imply that Christians may do anything in the name of winning persons to Christ? What are some of the positive aspects of this attitude? What are some of the pitfalls? What guidelines might you use upon which to base your decisions as to what is appropriate and what is not?

2. When the riot was incited in the Temple, Luke tells us that many of the spectators became like sheep following one another. Indeed, many of those present were not even certain what the conflict was all about. Do Christians ever join in a conflict without being certain of the issues involved? Name several examples. What do you

think makes us susceptible to such blind action? What remedies can you recommend?

3. Paul retells his conversion experience several times, each time as an attempt to convert others to faith in Jesus Christ. Have you ever related the story of your conversion as a way of telling others about the gospel? Are you comfortable in doing so, or in hearing others tell of their experiences? Do you think this is an effective way of winning others to the Christian faith?

4. When giving his witness, Paul uses what he considers relevant to those he is addressing. Although the basic story is the same, he adds or omits details depending on his audience. When you witness to others about your experience, are you sensitive to your audience? How might you adapt your witness to different situations?

5. Throughout his ministry, Paul exhibited extraordinary courage in the face of life-threatening situations. However, we are told that when Festus asked him if he was willing to return to Jerusalem for trial, the apostle became alarmed and appealed to Caesar, as was his right as a Roman citizen. How do you account for this uncharacteristic action by Paul? Was it a sudden attack of cowardice, or was there something more important involved?

6. Following his interview with Agrippa and Festus, Paul could have been set free; both officials knew that he was innocent. However, because he had appealed to Caesar, they had no choice but to send him to Rome. Do you think that Paul may have regretted his decision? Would the ultimate result have been the same in Jerusalem as in Rome? Do you feel that God was at work in these particular circumstances? Why or why not?

7. Throughout his missionary travels, Paul consistently preached the gospel to the Jews, gave them an opportunity to respond, then turned to the gentiles. In view of the fact that his mission to the Jews continually met with

failure, why do you suppose he persisted in this pattern? Do you think he might have been more effective if he had simply concentrated on evangelizing the gentiles in the first place? What implications might this have for Christians today?

ABOUT THE AUTHOR

WILLIAM R. CANNON is a bishop of the United Methodist church retired from episcopal duties. Bishop Cannon presided over the Raleigh, Richmond, and Atlanta Episcopal Areas during his career as a bishop. Before his election to the episcopacy in 1968, Bishop Cannon served as Professor of Church History and then Dean of Chandler School of Theology at Emory University in Atlanta. He has also pastored churches in Atlanta and Oxford, Georgia.

Bishop Cannon's major recreation is travel. He has made close to one hundred trips abroad. Many of his travels have been to the holy land, tracing the missionary journeys of Paul. Bishop Cannon has visited every site mentioned in the book of Acts.

Other books of Bible study by William R. Cannon include *The Gospel of John* and *Jesus the Servant* on the Gospel of Mark.